A Good Death

~~∞~~

IRENE S. SWITANKOWSKY

A Good Death
Copyright © 2018 by Irene S. Switankowsky

All rights reserved. No part of this publication may be reproduced, distributed, or transmitted in any form or by any means, including photocopying, recording, or other electronic or mechanical methods, without the prior written permission of the author, except in the case of brief quotations embodied in critical reviews and certain other non-commercial uses permitted by copyright law.

Tellwell Talent
www.tellwell.ca

ISBN
978-1-77370-307-7 (Paperback)
978-1-77370-308-4 (eBook)

Table of Contents

Introduction...................................3

Chapter 1: The Nature of Death and Dying 11

Chapter 2: Patient-Related Problems
When Dealing With End-of-Life Care 21

Chapter 3: Physician-Related Problems
with End-of-Life Care 29

Chapter 4: Empathic Physician-Patient
Communication 39

Chapter 5: Effective Physician-Patient
Understanding.................................47

Chapter 6: Rational Decision-Making 57

Chapter 7: Developing an Effective
Physician-Patient Relationship 69

Chapter 8: Shared Decision Making................77

Chapter 9: Accepting the Unpredictable Nature
of With End-of-Life Care.........................85

Chapter 10: A Humane Patient-Centered
Approach to End-of-Life Care....................93

Bibliography..................................100

Notes: 109

PART I:

AN INTRODUCTION TO END-OF-LIFE CARE

Introduction

When we think of the idea of *good death*, it resembles an oxymoron on the surface. What can there be that is possibly good about death? That's a good question! Therefore, it is important to reframe the question a bit and rethink the whole idea of *good death*. This will be the focus on this book.

For over two decades, I have been advocating a patient-centered approach to medical care. My first book focused on what constituted an informed consent in medical practise, in general. I argued to achieve an informed consent, a physician must utilize the patient-centered approach. Then in the early and mid-2000's I applied the patient-centered framework to terminally-ill and geriatric patients.

Now that Bill C-14, the Euthanasia and Assisted Suicide Bill has been passed, it is urgent to revisit the patient-centered approach and end-of-life care. I believe that the patient-centered approach can offer patients the hope of achieving a good death. Without this approach, physicians and other medical staff cannot ensure that patients will experience a good death, without imposing some version of mercy killing.

Actively killing patients, even those who are suffering greatly, is against the Hippocratic Oath which states the following:

> I swear by Apollo Physician and Asclepius and Hygieia and Panaceia and all the gods and goddesses, making them my witnesses, that I will fulfil according to my ability and judgment this oath and this covenant:
>
> To hold him who has taught me this art as equal to my parents and to live my life in partnership with him, and if he is in need of money to give him a share of mine, and to regard his offspring as equal to my brothers in male lineage and to teach them this art - if they desire to learn it - without fee and covenant; to give a share of precepts and oral instruction and all the other learning to my sons and to the sons of him who has instructed me and to pupils who have signed the covenant and have taken an oath according to the medical law, but no one else.
>
> I will apply dietetic measures for the benefit of the sick according to my ability and judgment; I will keep them from harm and injustice.
>
> I will neither give a deadly drug to anybody who asked for it, nor will I make a suggestion to this effect. Similarly I will not give to a woman an

abortive remedy. In purity and holiness I will guard my life and my art.

I will not use the knife, not even on sufferers from stone, but will withdraw in favor of such men as are engaged in this work.

Whatever houses I may visit, I will come for the benefit of the sick, remaining free of all intentional injustice, of all mischief and in particular of sexual relations with both female and male persons, be they free or slaves.

What I may see or hear in the course of the treatment or even outside of the treatment in regard to the life of men, which on no account one must spread abroad, I will keep to myself, holding such things shameful to be spoken about.

If I fulfil this oath and do not violate it, may it be granted to me to enjoy life and art, being honored with fame among all men for all time to come; if I transgress it and swear falsely, may the opposite of all this be my lot.

Here is a modern version of the Hippocratic Oath.

> I swear to fulfill, to the best of my ability and judgment, this covenant:
>
> I will respect the hard-won scientific gains of those physicians in whose steps I walk, and

gladly share such knowledge as is mine with those who are to follow.

I will apply, for the benefit of the sick, all measures which are required, avoiding those twin traps of overtreatment and therapeutic nihilism.

I will remember that there is art to medicine as well as science, and that warmth, sympathy, and understanding may outweigh the surgeon's knife or the chemist's drug.

I will not be ashamed to say, "I know not," nor will I fail to call in my colleagues when the skills of another are needed for a patient's recovery.

I will respect the privacy of my patients, for their problems are not disclosed to me that the world may know. Most especially must I tread with care in matters of life and death? If it is given me to save a life, all thanks. But it may also be within my power to take a life; this awesome responsibility must be faced with great humbleness and awareness of my own frailty. Above all, I must not play at God.

I will remember that I do not treat a fever chart, a cancerous growth, but a sick human being, whose illness may affect the person's family and economic stability. My responsibility includes these related problems, if I am to care adequately for the sick.

I will prevent disease whenever I can, for prevention is preferable to cure.

I will remember that I remain a member of society, with special obligations to all my fellow human beings, those of sound mind and body as well as the infirm.

If I do not violate this oath, may I enjoy life and art, respected while I live and remembered with affection thereafter. May I always act so as to preserve the finest traditions of my calling and may I long experience the joy of healing those who seek my help.

MY ANALYSIS OF THE HIPPOCRATIC OATH

So, given the wording in the Hippocratic Oath, which every physician swears to before, where does it say that active killing is permissible?

Frankly, I don't see it anywhere. In fact, I see quite the opposite in this passage:

> I will neither give a deadly drug to anybody who asked for it, nor will I make a suggestion to this effect. Similarly I will not give to a woman an abortive remedy. In purity and holiness, I will guard my life and my art.

So, then why do we continue to *pretend that it is permissible for physicians to kill patients who are at the end-of-life?*

One reason may be because we live in a culture where it seems to be permissible to kill people if they are suffering or dying. But do some of these physicians ever sit down and really talk with their patients about what they truly want, and feel is important with their end-of-life care?

I believe a patient-centered approach to end-of-life care can help physicians and medical staff to compassionately and humanely develop a unique end-of-life approach for each patient. Since every patient's life is unique, so should their end-of-life support be unique to him/her.

It is up to the medical staff and physicians to come up with a unique plan for each patient. How medical practitioners can do this best will be examined in detail throughout this book. In fact, I will spend a good half of the book going through the five principles of a patient-centered approach to caring for the dying. These principles, when applied consistently, will help patients experience a good death.

There are a lot of books on the market now about dying with dignity and death and aging because of the new Euthanasia and Assisted Suicide Bill that was recently passed in Ontario. In fact, much ink was spilled even before the passing of this bill because people were worried. And people are still worried, especially the elderly and vulnerable as well as the health practitioners who are worried about acquiescing with this Bill for moral or religious reasons. Some doctors feel very uncomfortable with this Bill because they don't want to end a patient's life for moral or religious reasons.

Also, this is a timely topic given that Quebec has already passed a Euthanasia law last year. I believe British Columbia is also on its way to passing a similar Bill. So, it seems that most of Canada will be moving in this very dangerous and frightening direction in time.

This is also a timely topic because there are more seniors than ever in history, and these numbers are going to only keep rising over the next twenty to thirty years. So, the time is right for this kind of Bill to be passed, given our already strapped medical system. But where does this leave the individual person and physician?

Have physicians and medical professionals overlooked the whole purpose of protecting their patients from eventual illness for as long as possible and help them live the best quality of life? Or perhaps, has the political system failed us? These questions must now be seriously addressed. Perhaps there be more emphasis on prevention and helping patients live the healthiest life possible so that patients can learn how to cope with different diseases?

Somehow the emphasis of medical staff and physicians has shifted away from honouring the dignity of the patient. It is important for medical professionals and lay people to start rethinking their duties and obligations. I believe physician-assisted suicide is a very complex problem and must be dealt with on many different levels. This also means that the onus is on patients to clearly communicate with their physicians. It can no longer solely be up to the physicians to keep probing.

In this book I will show the reader how to accomplish this one chapter at a time. I believe what is needed is a multi-pronged approach and ways of communicating to make the end-of-life care easier and more patient-specific.

CHAPTER 1

The Nature of Death and Dying

In many ways, death is a taboo topic. No one feels comfortable to talk about death. Most of us would like to pretend that it will never happen to us. And that is probably why we seem so focused on distracting ourselves from the realities of death, when the time draws nearer for all of us.

The truth is none of us can avoid death. This is a passage that we will all have to go through. It is a final passage, and because of this, it has tremendous negative connotations. But it is something we all inevitably must face.

Given our culture of secrecy about death, I believe the first step is to open discussion about death and dying so that we can be more comfortable talking about these end-of-life issues.

This lack of comfort about death especially resides in our families. For instance, when our parents are dying, many of us feel uncomfortable to even visit them. We prefer to play a disappearance act instead of facing the fact that our parent is dying and going to leave us shortly.

There's a rather older adage and it goes like this: There is a time for living, and there is a time for dying. When we are young, it is far easier not to think about death and dying. It is also easier not to think about suffering and pain. However, as we get older, this view changes as we start experiencing the odd pain here and there, and we start to experience a lot of chronic pain and fatigue. But that is all a part of life.

I believe that it is this lack of comfort with the idea of death and dying has brought about Bill C-14. Since we don't like to talk about death, why go through the long lingering process of dying. Just end the suffering fast. In other words, when matters get difficult, as they surely will eventually for all of us, perhaps it is easier to simply turn to mercy killing. Then you don't have to watch your loved one suffer, and you don't have to feel uncomfortable.

But is this really the answer to our problems with death and dying? I don't believe it does so because it just distracts us from the real issues at hand which still centers on our overall discomfort with death and dying. In addition, some physicians are even uncomfortable with the idea of death and dying. They are trained to cure and help people feel better. But when patients can no longer be helped, this can make them feel even more anxious and unhappy. It can also make physicians feel out of control.

But every illness and disease have a rhythm that cannot be controlled by anyone, not even doctors and medical interventions. It seems that there is a rhythm to our lives that no one can tinker with, not even medical experts.

So, what should physicians do? What should patients do? This is what I will spend the first part of the book discussing in detail. I believe we can all do our part to make the process of dying as good as it can be.

However, we have much work to do in accepting our health situation as it is. Ideally, if we practise the proper preventative techniques during our lives and live a life that is not too stressful and harmful to our health, we will probably not be as sick and disease prone as others who are reckless with their health.

Now there are many exceptions to this ideal. Some people may exercise, eat right, and live a healthy lifestyle, yet they still may get quite ill way before they should. This is because their genetics makes them more prone to certain illnesses and diseases. But also, the environment, pollutants, and what we ingest can play a key part.

However, it is still better to be proactive with your health and know that you did everything that you can to live a healthy and stress-free life as much as possible. Then you will have a better chance of experiencing good health during your older years.

However, like death and other serious issues, we don't want to be proactive with our health until we absolutely must do so. We rush from place to place. We are never content, much less happy. We overthink and overwork. We overdrink and overeat. We argue and don't get along, even with our own family members. Is it any wonder we get ill?

I believe that each of us has a choice on how to live. We can step back and decide what is important in our lives. For instance, do we really need that expensive house with ten rooms? Or, is a smaller house just as acceptable, one that we can afford? Do we need that $50,000 car, or is it just as acceptable to buy a $20,000 to $25,000 car that is reliable and affordable? Or, do you have to own an endless amount of clothes in your closet or can you buy a few new pieces a year (at most) and make the best of them?

I believe that the more complicated our lives become, and the more we expect to buy and get, the worse we will feel and the more stressed out. For one thing, we will have to work long hours to make ends meet. If we have a big house, our utilities will cost a lot more than if we lived in an average size home instead.

Also, do we use shopping as therapy? I always chuckle at the notion of shopping to make ourselves feel better. However, something that puts a smile on your face that is relatively cheap is acceptable from time to time. That way, it won't strain your pocketbook to the point that you must work more hours just to make ends meet, putting more stress and strain into your life. These stressors can have a negative impact on your health over time.

So, what can we do about this? I believe that we can create a comfortable life for ourselves if we are proactive about our health, enjoy the simple pleasures in life, and not overstress. This is indeed a recipe for good health and less suffering in the long run. And if we learn to accept our lives as they are at every stage, we'll be more likely to accept our end-of-life and ultimately death as well.

WHAT MAKES DEATH AND DYING DIFFICULT

There are several aspects of death which makes it especially difficult for physicians to effectively interact with the patient. The nature of medical practise is such that physicians usually treat patients for acute symptoms and come to some sort of resolution about a symptom and its treatment. That is the way acute conditions are usually dealt with quickly and easily. However, this is not an effective approach for patients who are ill and are dying because this time of life is plagued with ambiguity and uncertainty for the patient as well as the physician.

We must remember that there is no one resolution to death and dying because it is a multi-faceted issue. In addition, the nature of death is such that there is no one way of handling this time of life that fits all patients. This underscores the frustrating nature of dying, both for the patient and physician. All the physician can really do is to prescribe different pain medications and treatments that the patient can try. All the patient can do is to try to manage his/her pain and suffering at the moment.

This situation can especially frustrate physicians because many of them don't feel comfortable telling their dying patients that there is very little that they can do to help them. As mentioned before, *modern medical practice* is an area in which much can be done to help patients. Medical science has made many advances and have had breakthroughs for many serious diseases. People are living longer in relatively good health. This is because medicine is, at least in part, a science through which physical symptoms are improved through treatments or surgical procedures. To humanely treat dying patients, it is essential that physicians shift their focus from curing to compassionately caring for them.

Second, the nature of serious illness is unpredictable since a patient's illness won't go away. In fact, unfortunately it will usually keep getting worse. Physicians may sometimes feel as if they're hitting their head against an impenetrable wall of symptoms. In some cases, it's even difficult for a physician to know if the patient described his/her symptoms correctly. This is because some dying patients may have a difficult time describing their symptoms in measurable terms. Sometimes, words cannot even accurately capture how they feel. So, neither physicians nor patients can help each other dispel the ambiguous components of old age. This can hinder effective communication and fragment the physician-patient encounter, as I will discuss in Part II.

This last stage of a patient's life is usually a time that is riddled with disease which can continue for many years without improving, causing increasing pain and suffering. How a patient reacts to this pain and suffering depends on many conditions.

First, the severity of the disabilities and suffering caused by the disease can make a substantial difference on how the patient copes. For instance, if a patient cannot walk without pain, (s)he will have a hard time coping with his/her disease.

Second, patients who are in constant pain because of the disease will put all their time and energy into finding relief from everyday symptoms. They may not have any extra energy to cope effectively with the psychological ramifications of their illness.

Third, patients who lack social support do not fare well either. Thus, patients must develop different social support networks to help them cope with their disabilities. This can help them cope as their disease keeps progressing.

Lastly, the patient's pre-illness personality can greatly affect the prognosis. For instance, if the patient has always been resilient before becoming ill, (s)he will probably be more positive and even hopeful after being diagnosed with the illness. However, if the patient's overall attitude was pessimistic before becoming ill and entering this last stage of life, (s)he may negatively cope with the onset of the illness.

The nature of death and dying is such that the patient will lose his/her immediate competency and be deprived of a pain-free future. A patient's future is usually marked by continual weakness and disability, which can cause the patient a lot of stress and uncertainty. Nothing is ever certain for the dying patient, except perhaps death itself. And this unpredictability can be difficult for a patient to bear over time. There doesn't seem to be any release from the malaise of continuous pain and disability and eventual death. Every day becomes an increasingly complex winding road leading to nowhere better.

As a result, dying patients can start feeling hopeless and helpless. Many patients feel useless and unable to even do the basic things in life. This can make the patient feel increasingly isolated and even depressed.

Instead of feeling helpless, the patient should strive to develop as positive an attitude as possible in relation to his/her disabilities. It is especially important for a patient to create and sustain a sense of inner tranquility in the face of these life-threatening difficulties.

However, to remain psychologically fit while physically in pain requires that patient come to believe that their personal worth goes beyond his/her physical limitations. This can give patients a more hopeful and positive approach to their illness. In other words, a patient needs to be self-empowered to truly adapt to his/her illness. Often by developing a state of equanimity and peace, the patient is better able to accept what is happening.

Fear can paralyze dying patients in other ways as well. Many patients are afraid of the future and because of this they may frame the rest of their lives in terms of death. Dying is not something that can be controlled by anyone and worrying about what *may* happen can be a waste of time and especially energy, given that the patient doesn't have much time anyways.

Thus, it is essential for dying patients to face their illness and live each day as fully as possible. If a patient is having a bad day, (s)he should be extra kind to him/herself by taking steps to give him/herself ample rest periods during the day and doing something she truly enjoys.

In addition, the patient should not let bad days get him/her down but instead take concrete steps to accept and cope with the symptoms. If a patient can develop and maintain a positive attitude, (s)he can better cope with his/her disabilities.

HOW A DYING PATIENT CAN FEEL MORE IN CONTROL

One important thing for a dying patient to do is to find ways to feel more in control of her illness. This seems to like a nonsensical idea on the surface since the patient is dying. What is there to control right? Well, this is true, but the good news is that there are small things a patient can do to feel hopeful and more in control, even if it is in just this moment. Here are four things dying patients can try.

First, the patient could educate him/herself about the disease she is living with. Its never too late to learn more about your condition. Knowledge is power and the more a patient can learn about his/her illness, the better (s)he will be able to cope. Every illness requires patients to learn how to adapt to his/her *version* of the disease. This is because every disease is patient-specific and must be properly accommodated by physicians. Therefore, it isn't surprising that the process of dying is also patient-specific, dependent on our temperament, mental health, and overall physical health.

Second, patients should learn how to manage their own illness and the unique challenges that it presents. It can be difficult for a newly diagnosed patient to moderate his/her life so that (s)he can positively live and cope with his/her disease and death. First and foremost, the patient must accept that her life will never be the same again. The patient will always have to amend his/her actions, behaviours, and especially lifestyle, to accommodate his/her new reality. There are quite a few different self-management techniques that patients can try to ease their pain and fatigue levels, such as using assistive devices, pacing themselves, lowering expectations, practising relaxation techniques, and putting certain stress-reducing mechanisms in place.

Third, patients may develop low self-esteem over time because of the continuous nature of pain and disability. This state of pain and pending death can make it difficult for a patient to feel positive and joyful. This negative feeling can also make it harder for the patient to accept his/her disease and medical situation.

Instead, patients should realize that they deserve to be hopeful. The patient should strive to develop positive self-esteem, which can be achieved by choosing to be hopeful in the face of obstacles and the basic challenges of life, and to have a positive image of oneself and realize that one has a basic right to be happy.

Lastly, patients should learn how to positively adapt to the physical and psychological symptoms of their illness and the dying process. This is probably the most difficult part of coping with end-of-life issues. When a patient is diagnosed with a serious illness, as time passes, (s)he won't be able to do the things (s)he used to.

Because of this, the patient will feel frustrated and angry. But by learning to live as comfortably as possible and developing a positive attitude, patients can still experience a good quality of life. We all deserve to be happy. Therefore, patients must ensure that their illness does not destroy the quality of their remaining time.

In this chapter, I examined the nature of dying and how dying patients can ensure that they do their part to take care of themselves as much as possible. The process of death and dying is patient-specific and because of this, different patients will cope with it differently.

One of the purposes of this chapter was to encourage patients to take charge of their illness in positive ways, as much as this is possible. Dying patients don't have to simply wait for things to get worse before they learn how to positively cope with their illness. Instead, they can learn to be hopeful to preserve the quality of their remaining life.

CHAPTER 2

Patient-Related Problems When Dealing With End-of-Life Care

Many dying patients find it difficult to be proactive about different aspects of their health and lives. Patients feel out of control and angry. Further, many patients live in a perpetual state of *the crisis stage*. During this stage, the patient often feels hopeless and frightened about the future.

But what does it really mean to control our end-of-life care? Can advance directives that we drew up years prior have the same kind of authority as they had before? Do patients have the right to terminate their lives if their life becomes unbearable? Who gets to choose when enough is enough?

Many Canadians believe that we should have autonomy over our death. That is why there was such an urgent move to decriminalize physician-assisted death in Ontario and other provinces in Canada. However, there are so many thorny issues left unaddressed for both the patient and physician despite the seeming freedom about their lives that patients now have from Bill C-14.

This is because the idea of death and dying are very hard for patients to face. It isn't easy for patients to say with any kind of certainty that my life is no longer worth living because I am suffering greatly. Not surprisingly, many times at the end-of-life, the patient's views are framed in terms of suffering and the lack of control that they feel in their lives.

Many patients in their last years live in retirement homes or they are shut-ins. Many feel isolated and depressed. How on earth can they make rational decisions about their end-of-life care? There seems to be so much going wrong, and they are always enduring so much suffering. Often, their family is no longer visiting them as often, and many of them feel like a burden to everyone.

I believe it can be difficult for a patient in this situation to make a rational end-of-life decision about her health care on his/her own. For this reason, I believe patients should call on other medical care workers and physicians who they can talk about their end-of-life care and where they can go from here. Then the physician, in collaboration with the patient, can decide on the best end-of-life care possible, one that is congruent with the patient's values and beliefs, and ideally one that the patient can feel comfortable with.

DEALING WITH SHORT-TERM SYMPTOMS AT THE END-OF-LIFE

In the short–term, however, patients must learn to effectively deal with the symptoms of their illness so that their end-of-life can be as pain-free as possible. To deal with the physical symptoms and control the psychological ramifications of the illness, the patient must:

1. Comply with the treatments prescribed by the physician and other medical specialists;
2. Accept the illness and not be in denial about it;
3. Honestly deal with the psychological ramifications of the illness; and
4. Develop self-management techniques to help cope with the effects of the illness as effectively as possible.

By following these steps, dying patients will be living as healthy and pain-free as possible. I will explain each of these components in more detail below.

(1) Dying patients should comply with all the treatments that the physician and other health experts prescribe. This can be a murky area for many patients because some individuals don't really understand the purpose of some of the treatments prescribed. For the treatments and medications to be helpful, however, patients MUST take their medications EXACTLY as prescribed by the physician.

Further, if the physician prescribes other treatments, such as physiotherapy to ease pain and increase mobility, the patient must follow-through on the physician's advice. By precisely following the treatments prescribed by a patient's health care team, (s)he will be taking the necessary steps to manage the symptoms of his/her disease and gain control over the pain and disability (s)he experiences.

Many patients, either intentionally or unintentionally, fail to follow through on a physician's verbal advice. This can be detrimental to a patient's success in effectively coping with her illness. Patients should remember that their physicians are experts and therefore their advice should be followed to the letter.

(2) In addition, patients must accept their illness and decide to take realistic steps to cope with it so that their quality of life is not negatively impacted. Patients may be in denial about their illness, especially when they are first diagnosed, but this does not help with their overall situation.

Instead, patients should accept their illness as an obstacle that must always be dealt with directly. Then, patients should move forward knowing that, although they can't change their overall diagnosis, they can control how they react to it by learning how to most effectively deal with the symptoms.

The worse thing a patient can do is to be in denial about his/her illness. Having an illness can involve an emotional roller coaster ride for many patients since they may not be able to move or live as they did at the onset of the illness or get nearly as much accomplished.

Thus, patients will have to curb their previous activities and pace themselves in order not to suffer from overwhelming amounts of pain and fatigue. Illness can zap a patient's overall physical and psychological vitality. However, patients can take steps to live a good quality of life by reprioritizing their daily activities and pacing themselves.

(3) Often, in the last stages of life, patients often suffer from bouts of depression, anxiety, or even anger. Sadly, during this stage of life, it is as normal for the patient to

experience depression as having physical disabilities. Therefore, it is important for patients to develop proper coping mechanisms for bad days. This way, patients wouldn't be negatively impacted by different forms of psychological distress that is related to their illness. A dying patient can often become quite overwhelmed on many different levels. That feeling usually occurs when the patient can't take care of him/herself as (s)he used to. However, there are quite a few things patients can do to feel more in control of their illness.

(4) Further, dying patients can gain control over their symptoms by planning for activities that take a great deal of energy. For instance, it is natural for a patient to feel angry after realizing that (s)he no longer has as much energy to do the same things as (s)he used to.

In such a case, a patient should try to manage his/her busier days by planning so that (s)he doesn't become totally exhausted and experience extreme pain as a result. Or, if a patient has a dinner party coming up, (s)he should start preparing for the event a few weeks ahead of time. By pacing and taking frequent breaks, the patient can better control the symptoms of the terminal illness.

Second, a patient can gain control over the symptoms of his/her illness by turning negative thoughts about the illness and how she feels into positive ones. As much as possible, the patient should try not to negatively bias her view of life by framing it in terms of death. This can be hard to do at first; however, once the panic of the initial diagnosis subsides a bit, then a patient can incorporate small changes into his/her life that will lessen his/her pain and discomfort levels over time. This can improve the quality of the individual's life over time as well.

Third, the patient should learn problem-solving techniques to help resolve some of his/her daily pains and discomforts. One of the first steps is for a patient to determine what his/her health disabilities are, brainstorm solutions, and try one solution for two weeks to see if it helps improve pain and disability levels. This will ensure that the patient gains more self-control over his/her illness. There are solutions to most of a patient's problems if (s)he only can take the time to discover them with an open and hopeful mind.

HOW TO COPE WITH RECEIVING A LIFE-ALTERING DIAGNOSIS

There is nothing worse than receiving news that one has a serious life-altering disease. The initial panic that a patient and his/her family feels is mind boggling. There is a state of heightened anxiety and stress that ensures in the days, weeks and months of a patient's life.

Yet, we will all eventually receive a dire diagnosis from a doctor in our lifetimes if we live long enough. We will all experience this angst and overwhelming urge to scream and recoil into a dark vortex of negative feelings and emotions. But is this how we want to end our lives?

I would hope not. But it can be very hard not to fall into this negative frame of mind at least initially. After all, we are dying. And there is nothing we can do about that, it seems. So, what is there to do? We may as well give up, right? Well, no, we don't have to give up or recoil. Here are a few things you can do to feel more in control of your situation.

First, you should try to be in habitual contact with others. It can be especially difficult to deal with your situation if you live in isolation. Therefore, join a support group of people who are in the last stages of life. There is no better feeling than knowing that you are not alone in your predicament.

Second, try to deepen your personal relationships with family and friends. Your family will be in shock after your diagnosis. But if you make it a point to talk to them and spend time with them they may not feel as panic-ridden. Thus, it is important to open lines of communication with your family.

Third, try to do the things that you love as often as possible. Don't waste time dwelling on the inevitable. But instead, choose one or two things that you love to do and do them every day. This should help lift your spirits.

Fourth, read the books that you always wanted to. Spend time reading and explore topics that you never did. It is never too late to learn new things. This may even give you some new perspective and it is a great way of moving into the world of an author for a few hours here and there.

Fifth, try to commune with nature every day. You may want to take a brief walk or just get in your backyard or sit on your patio. Sip a tall cool glass of water and enjoy your surroundings. Listen to the birds. Feel the wind on your skin. Look at the different shades of green in the trees and shrubs.

Sixth, live in the moment as much as possible. All we have is this moment. So, why waste time wondering what will happen. Just focus on right now and making this moment the best that it can be. This should lighten your spirit and allow you to enjoy the quality of your life.

By taking these steps, you will be more than just coping with your terminal illness. You will also be enjoying your life one day at a time and one moment at a time. Because this is all that any of us have for sure—this very moment now.

As we saw in this chapter, there are many patient-related problems to receiving a serious, life-altering diagnosis. However, once the initial shock subsides, there are a lot of things we can do to help ourselves cope by living the best quality of life possible.

CHAPTER 3

Physician-Related Problems with End-of-Life Care

Most diagnosis and treatments in medical practice are measured by some scientific evidence. Yet, terminal disease and pending death doesn't lend itself to such a scientific formulation of treatment options.

Because of this, physicians may find it difficult to prescribe treatments that involve measurable kinds of assessments since there is no guarantee that these treatments and medications will help a dying patient. In some cases, these treatments may make the patient feel worse.

But what is more, monitoring the exact progress of such treatments can be especially difficult too. Such unpredictable treatment results can frustrate the physician, given the typically predictable nature of medical practice, making it difficult to determine whether (s)he is helping the patient in any significant way. The unpredictable nature of caring for a dying patient is very different in nature from acutely-ill patients since there is no one-size-fits-all solutions to alleviate the symptoms of the illness.

Thus, the process of treating a dying patient can be time consuming and especially costly for several reasons. First, dying patients must be booked for longer appointment times because their symptoms are not always clear cut. The physician may also realize that, for some patients, the symptoms can be psychosomatic, further complicating the clinical encounter.

In addition, some dying patients may be afraid and depressed. Sadly, serious illness doesn't usually miraculously get better. Rather, the disease usually gets worse over time. This can negatively affect the overall morale of the patient and the clinical encounter. It can also make it difficult for the patient to become proactive with the years or months that are left because of how hopeless (s)he feels. The patient's whole life will be framed in terms of death.

Second, it may be difficult for the physician to effectively probe into the causes of the illness because they are not always straightforward. The physician must usually ask questions about the patient's family background and life circumstances. This can take time, effort, and a lot of detective work. It can also be hampered by the vague descriptions of the patient's symptoms. Many times, the patient's symptoms defy accurate description and measurement.

Third, serious end-of-life illness is usually unobservable, and the symptoms are largely immeasurable. Many dying patients don't have any outward physical manifestations of sickness. They mostly look like normal and healthy people. The difficulty with experiencing unobservable symptoms is that the physician cannot always get an accurate sense of the pain, disability, and discomfort that the patient is experiencing at any time. In addition, the pain experienced is often subjective and patient-specific, adding to the ambiguity of providing adequate treatment options.

For instance, having a serious illness that leads to death over time is not like having a broken leg that requires surgery or treatment. Once the leg is healed, the pain tends to disappear, and the patient can resume his/her normal life. For most dying patients, however, the pain lingers for many months or even years. In addition, most times, patients have a difficult time precisely describing their pain or pointing to where it is located. Sometimes, the pain experienced seems to be all over the body.

Further, there is little that a physician can prescribe to substantially help the patient's overall pain levels or quality of life. In other words, there is no *magic bullet* to alleviate pain and suffering once and for all. This can be especially frustrating for the patient who is hoping to get a bit of relief from their pain.

Thus, there are very few evidence-based guidelines that physicians can rely on to treat dying patients. For instance, since a patient's pain levels are largely patient-specific and based on individual tolerances, it is difficult for the physician to accurately assess just how much pain a patient is experiencing at any given time.

Instead, physicians must rely on the patient's subjective report of pain. And this report can be biased when a patient is dying because the patient will feel especially hopeless.

Therefore, physicians may treat pain as something that is normal, given the patient's diagnosis, which can further complicate their interaction with dying patients. This can also create a breach in trust which can result in the physician-patient relationship being seriously hampered.

To remedy this situation, I believe that the physician should rely on another paradigm of medical care to treat dying patients, one that is based on the qualitative aspects of the medical care. This is where the patient-centered approach to be outlined in Part II is not only relevant, but necessary. The **five** conditions of the patient-centered approach should facilitate the physician-patient encounter and make it even more wholesome and meaningful both for the patient and physician.

THE FIVE CONDITIONS OF THE PATIENT-CENTERED APPROACH

The patient-centered approach gives the dying patient precedence in a medical interaction. It is an approach that is empathic to a patient's concerns and overall well-being. Because this approach is largely patient-based, it is much less measurable and much more subjective than your typical clinical encounter.

I believe including the subjective components of terminal illness when treating dying patients is not only necessary but required for humane health care. The nature of terminal illness is so difficult for patients to get their heads around that physicians must treat the whole patient not only the disease itself. Serious illness makes patients vulnerable and uncertain, and physicians must try to address such immeasurable concerns during the clinical encounter.

The five conditions of the patient-centered approach to be discussed in Part II highlight these subjective concerns. The five principles focus on developing a humane, empathic, open, honest, and trusting relationship with a dying patient so that she can make rational decisions for or against treatment. These five principles will also help the physician come to terms with the unpredictable nature of terminal illness.

Here is a brief synopsis of the five conditions of the patient-centered approach to be discussed in more detail in Part II.

The first condition requires that the physician **engage in empathic communication with the dying patient**. This ultimately requires that the physician understand the patient and develop a trusting relationship with him/her. Trust can help physicians mend the communication gaps that may exist between themselves and their patients. To develop trust, the patient should feel comfortable to openly discuss any of his/her symptoms to the physician, and the physician should seek to understand the patient's predicament, despite the fact some of the symptoms may defy accurate measurement.

The second condition encourages physicians to effectively **understand their patients.** Understanding is one of the most important principles which physicians can display to dying patients during the clinical encounter. The nature of serious illness is such that it is difficult for the patient to always feel supported and cared for due to the constant pain and discomfort she feels.

Many dying patients may even become depressed and feel hopeless. Because of the dying patient's vulnerabilities, it is essential for the physician to try and *imagine what it would be like* to experience constant pain and fatigue that is like what the patient is always feeling. Then the physician can more effectively help the patient.

The **third** condition is rational decision making. It can be hard for seriously ill patients to make a rational, unbiased decision about treatment. Usually, upon hearing the diagnosis, the patient feels hopeless. This hopelessness can translate into biased decisions that are out of character for the patient. Such biased decisions result in uninformed nonautonomous, decisions. This is something that patients should avoid.

The **fourth** condition encourages the physician and patient to develop an effective physician-patient relationship so that they can engage in open, honest communication. The physician can do this by developing an open and honest relationship. To do so, the physician must spend a considerable amount of time attentively listening to the patient to understand how the patient is coping, given the symptoms of his/her life-threatening illness. It's never easy to develop an open, honest relationship with a patient who may be depressed and down on life, especially when the physician knows that (s)he can never completely alleviate the patient's pain and discomfort.

The nature of medical practice is such that physicians are used to treating patients and alleviating pain. And for most patients, except the dying, this is indeed possible. However, the dying patient presents a distinct set of challenges for the physician.

The fifth condition highlights the importance of **shared or mutual decision-making between physician and patient.** Shared decision-making occurs when the physician, along with the patient, tries to make a mutual decision about a treatment option or surgery. It can be difficult for dying patients to make effective decisions on their own. Many times, dying patients will make biased decisions for or against a treatment based on subjective feelings. Many patients don't want to accept treatments because they frame the decision in terms of their pending death.

It is, therefore, important for the physician to ***guide*** such patients into a much more rational and unbiased decisions by helping them to realize that certain treatments and/or surgeries can make the quality of their lives so much better. Many dying patients may frame the benefits of treatments in terms of the drawbacks involved instead of the benefits that may ensue. This can also hinder the patient from making rational decisions about their treatment options which may help him/her feel less pain in the long run.

Thus, physicians must develop a humane patient-centered approach for each dying patient. This will help physicians feel less frustrated and more accepting of the unpredictable nature of medical care that must be administered for dying patients.

In Part II, I will examine these five conditions of the patient-centered approach for the dying patient in detail. I will argue that once these conditions are met by physicians, they will be able to treat dying patients in a humane manner. In addition, the patient-centered approach will help physicians develop a type of medical care that is best suited to the dying patient.

PART II

THE FIVE CONDITIONS OF THE PATIENT-CENTERED APPROACH OF END OF LIFE CARE

CHAPTER 4

Empathic Physician-Patient Communication

The first condition of the patient-centered approach is empathic physician-patient communication. An important part of the patient-centered approach for the dying is for the physician and patient to learn how to communicate clearly and compassionately with one another about the patient's concerns. Every terminally-ill patient will have unique challenges to cope with because of his/her illness. It is, therefore, important for physicians to try and help patients feel more at ease.

Patients must also be encouraged to take charge of their health, despite having a terminal illness. So, **empathic physician-patient communication** is required to bring about humane health care because it is among the most important aspects of caring for a terminally-ill patient. The patient-centered approach makes the patient's concerns a top priority in every medical encounter. This approach can help a patient feel empowered and encouraged at a time when (s)he may feel the most vulnerable, fearful, anxious, and out of control.

There are three dimensions of empathic communication. These are as follows:

   I. Developing open and honest communication;
  II. A discussion of the patient's fears; and
 III. Empathy with the patient's predicament.

Each of these three dimensions of communication are beneficial in helping the terminally-ill patient to more readily accept and deal with his or her situation. These dimensions can also help the patient overcome the overwhelming frustration and anxiety of living with a terminal condition.

I. DEVELOPING OPEN, HONEST COMMUNICATION

When the patient is diagnosed with a terminal illness, the physician should determine the most effective way to communicate with the patient about that illness based on the patient's specific needs. Each patient's needs will be different and unique in the final stages of his/her life. The medical encounter should, therefore, be such that the patient feels comfortable enough to ask questions and seek clarifications about treatments and other medical interventions.

In addition, the physician should carefully listen to a patient's avowals of pain and discomfort. The physician should try to fill in any grey areas in their discussion, with the patient's help. Grey areas occur when the patient is unable to clearly explain his/her symptoms or the frequency of them. The physician should not negatively judge a patient's questions and categorize them as trivial. Every question is acceptable because it reveals that patient's *unique* concerns and worries about the nature of his/her terminal illness and how it will impact the rest of his/her life.

There are two central components of empathic communication, *openness* and *honesty*, both of which are similar and yet distinct to a certain degree. Many psychologists and philosophers categorize *openness* as an aspect of *honesty*. However, the two concepts don't mean the same thing and should be separated to clearly distinguish between them during a clinical encounter.

On the one hand, *openness* typically has a psychological and subjective function in communication while *honesty* has a much more objective function. When a physician is *open* with the terminally-ill patient, (s)he allows a patient to express any emotions and fears that the patient might experience about the terminal illness.

In addition, the physician can express *openness* towards the patient through gestures and body language. When a physician is *honest*, (s)he usually more objectively discusses how a terminal illness will affect the rest of a patient's life. To be fully honest with the patient, the physician should disclose the results of his/her diagnosis in detail, without withholding any aspect of it.

In addition, the physician can express *openness* towards the patient through gestures and body language. Therefore, *honesty* also has an objective component. For instance, after running a few X-rays, the physician may discover that the patient has more inflammation or cancer cells in other parts of the body. It is important for the physician to disclose this fact to the patient. Terminal illness can present a lot of puzzling physical manifestations for patients, such as polyps or cysts in different areas of the body. These should also be disclosed to the patient.

Therefore, the subjective aspects of *openness* require that the physician provide the patient sufficient time to decide whether she wants to undergo a medical procedure, after the initial communication. This is especially the case for more invasive surgeries or treatments with a lot of negative side effects. The physician may also want to meet with the patient a few days or a week after the initial disclosure of the illness to determine whether there are any other matters that have surfaced and answer any further questions. Each terminally-ill patient has a unique way of coping with the diagnosis and treatment. Thus, the physician should determine how much consultation time is necessary for each patient.

One way to convey an *open* attitude is for the physician to sit closer to the patient when disclosing the diagnosis so that the physician can comfort the patient, if need be. This gesture usually helps to show a sense of emotional openness and comfort to the patient. Another way to be open towards the patient is for the physician to speak in a low, comforting tone of voice by using empathic and reassuring language when discussing the illness such as:

> *"I know this must be hard for you to cope with."*
> *"It must be hard to live with so much pain all the time."*

> *"It must be hard to receive this diagnosis. Please contact me anytime with questions and concerns. I am here for you."*

This will help the patient feel understood and encouraged to carry on, despite the patient's pain and suffering which the terminal illness poses daily.

II. AN OPEN DISCUSSION OF THE PATIENT'S FEARS

After the disclosure of diagnosis and possible treatment options, the physician must also leave a sufficient amount of time to discuss the patient's fears about the future. A patient diagnosed with a terminal illness is usually plagued with all kinds of fears and uncertainties. Most times, family members are not available, either physically or psychologically, to talk openly with the patient because they are also in a state of shock.

Also, many families do not often talk about their deepest concerns openly. So, the patient may refrain from telling the family members the whole truth about his/her medical situation until (s)he absolutely must.

Another way the physician could encourage the terminally-ill patient to talk about his/her fears is by asking open-ended questions such as: *How have you felt since the diagnosis? Can you keep working part-time? Which hobbies do you want to keep doing, despite the pain and fatigue? Do you feel a lot of pain? Does your pain medication help alleviate enough of your pain so that you can function properly and work?*

This type of probing process is especially important for patients who may have a difficult time effectively communicating with the physician. Some patients don't know where to start or how to voice their concerns. Many patients haven't spoken to anyone about their concerns and difficulties, so they don't even know how to effectively communicate about them concisely. By asking open-ended questions, the physician will engage the patient and hopefully make it easier for him/her to openly discuss his/her fears.

III. EMPATHY WITH A PATIENT'S PREDICAMENT

Empathy is another important feature of effective communication. Many times, the patient may feel insufficiently cared for. Terminal illness can make a patient feel more sensitive and vulnerable. Empathy shows a terminally-ill patient that the physician genuinely cares about his/her medical predicament.

In the process of empathic listening, a physician should listen carefully to the patient's questions and concerns. The physician must also try to understand the patient's feelings, determine the meaning of the patient's fears, and encourage the patient to reframe his/her negative attitudes towards the terminal illness.

In other words, an empathic physician must sense, intuit, and empathize with a patient's predicament as much as possible. To show empathy, the physician should genuinely feel sorry for the patient's situation and do everything medically possible to help the patient. Sympathy alone is insufficient to help a terminally ill patient cope with the effects of a terminal condition since sympathy merely involves feeling sorry for the patient. Instead, empathy shows the patient that the physician genuinely cares about his/her struggles and can put him/herself in the patient's shoes.

Empathy is, therefore, essential to bring about a humanistic, patient-centered encounter between physician and patient in her last stages of life. The physician should imagine what it would be like to experience the pain and disability the patient feels. Empathy is best understood as a tool which will assist in understanding the patient's predicament—not merely the feelings of communion or fellow-feeling with the other person, as would be the case with a sympathetic response to the patient.

Therefore, for the terminally-ill patient, a medical assessment should be combined with the patient-centered approach to best treat a patient. Any terminal illness negatively impacts the quality of a patient's life daily. The difference between a strictly medical conceptualization of terminal illness as a disease and the patient's interpretation as a lived experience of the illness which affects every aspect of his/her life, highlights the reason why the patient and physician may find it so difficult to effectively communicate with one another about his/her physical and especially psychophysical struggles. The physician's approach is mostly objective while the patient's is subjective. The patient-centered approach tries to soften this dichotomy between the subjective and objective approaches to illness by encouraging the physician to show more empathy and in every clinical encounter.

Thus, empathic communication is the foundation for achieving patient-centered care for the terminally-ill. Without empathic communication not only will the physician-patient relationship be hampered but the interaction between the two parties will be detached and impersonal. One important condition of a patient-centered approach is that a terminally-ill patient requires an empathic encounter between physician and patient to most effectively deal with his/her medical situation. This will lay the foundation of trust and acceptance that is necessary for the physician to help the patient effectively cope with the illness. In addition, an empathic encounter is a foundational element of the four conditions of the patient-centered approach to be discussed in the chapters that follow.

CHAPTER 5

Effective Physician-Patient Understanding

The second condition of the patient-centered approach is effective physician-patient understanding during the clinical encounter. Understanding requires a multi-staged analysis by the physician to determine that the patient indeed understands all the information disclosed about the diagnosis and prognosis and that she can make a rational decision about the best course of treatment, given her terminal illness. In this chapter, I will outline this process, detailing some of the difficulties inherent in shared understanding.

Terminally-ill patients are in a category of their own. They are unlike any other patient that the physician will treat. One important condition of a patient-centered approach to end-of-life care is to ensure that the physician fully understands the patient's difficulties and disabilities. This isn't always easy to achieve, given the ambiguities of terminal illness and the difficulty of getting a clear sense of the patient's needs. However, by trying to understand the patient's concerns, the physician can bring about a patient-centered approach to treating his/her patient.

BRINGING ABOUT EFFECTIVE UNDERSTANDING

An effective disclosure of a diagnosis requires that the patient understands the diagnosis, prognosis, and treatments outlined by the physician. Generally, an effective disclosure is an exchange between two individuals that has the overriding purpose of presenting information clearly and assisting understanding. Understanding may be characterized as the physician's assimilation of the information about a patient's illness and life situation and his/her understanding of the treatment options available. The criteria for understanding the disclosure of a diagnosis are complex since these involve psychological and intellectual idiosyncrasies which are unique to each patient. Each patient's degree and level of understanding must be intuitively assessed by the physician.

Several factors may be instrumental in ensuring that a medical disclosure is properly understood by the patient. First, according to the patient-centered model, a terminally-ill patient must *substantially* understand the diagnosis, prognosis, and communication about the treatments available to him/herself. A substantial amount of information is usually disclosed by the physician about the possible treatments available to the patient. Some of the types of medical information that may be disclosed include the diagnosis, all the risks and benefits for each treatment, the side effects for each treatment, and a ranking of the benefits of each treatment.

Second, each of these factors requires a detailed analysis. To make this information clear, the physician should schedule some extra time for the patient to process the information. This is especially the case for ranking the benefits of each treatment since the assessment usually requires an analysis and prioritization of the treatments available. This process requires that the patient can properly assimilate all the information disclosed. Understanding this information can be a complex process, depending on the patient's ability to understand the information disclosed by the physician.

THE THREE CONDITIONS OF EFFECTIVE UNDERSTANDING

Thus, as you can see, understanding between physician and patient is quite a complicated process. It involves clear understanding and shared nuances that only the patient can provide. In this section, I will outline and discuss the three conditions of understanding. These are: (1) Shared understanding; (2) Determining the relevancy of information disclosed; and (3) Using medical jargon sparingly.

(1) There is an important difference between *shared understanding* and *ordinary understanding*. *Shared understanding* is based on a reciprocal understanding between the physician and patient. *Ordinary understanding*, on the other hand, merely consists of communicating the facts, and the risks and benefits for each treatment, without attempting to take the patient's personal needs, values, and situation into consideration. It

is insufficient for the physician to simply communicate the raw facts and the risks and benefits of the treatments to the patient since the treatments will feel impersonal to the patient. Instead, the physician must personalize how she presents the treatments and their risks.

Shared understanding takes place when the physician understands the details of the patient's values, goals, beliefs, and life plans in relation to her illness. The physician then must operate within certain medical constraints which are, in effect, beyond his/her control. Both the physician and patient must, therefore, comprehend each other in a subjective, person-to-person manner, which allows each of them to openly and honestly communicate without manipulation or disingenuousness. The terminally-ill patient's feelings of grief and vulnerability can be greatly eased with such a shared understanding.

(2) Initially, the physician must reveal all the treatments available, without prioritizing them so that the ***relevancy of the information disclosed*** can be determined by the physician and patient. Then both the patient and physician should eliminate the irrelevant treatments, evaluating the remaining alternatives in greater detail. It should never merely be the physician's sole responsibility to decide which treatments are relevant to a patient. Relevancy is difficult to establish right away because it is usually unique to the patient. The unique personal and psychological manifestations of a terminal illness are difficult to unravel without communicating with the patient at length. Ensuring that a terminally-ill patient is included in the process of choosing the relevant treatments invites that patient into the decision-making process for treating his/her own illness. This, in turn, ensures that the

patient feels more in control of his/her terminal illness. This kind of shared decision-making also ensures that the patient is competent to decide which treatments are best to schedule soon and which to forgo.

(3) ***If the treatments are disclosed to the patient using strictly medical terminology***, (s)he will not be able to fully understand the disclosure. Medical terminology is usually considered to be a convenient short-hand; but when communicating with a patient, these treatments should be translated into ordinary language so that the patient is able to understand. The patient has no medical training, and although most patients are better informed about health matters today than a few decades ago, technical medical jargon can still make it impossible for most patients to effectively understand the disclosure. Thus, the physician should be extremely careful about how much medical jargon she uses when disclosing information about the treatments available.

Different patients have different capacities for understanding. Some patients are more informed and better able to understand physicians. Other patients have a difficult time understanding the treatments disclosed by the physician. The degree of difficulty in understanding can depend on many different factors. Some of these are as follows: (a) Levels of education; (b) Capacities for reflectiveness; and (c) Psychological factors, such as (i) relentless pain; (ii) feelings of hopelessness and depression; and (iii) denial.

a. Differing levels of education affect how, or even whether, a patient will grasp and understand the medical information disclosed by the physician. In addition, there will be a difference in how long a patient takes to comprehend the medical information provided by the physician. terminally-ill patients with secondary and post-secondary education do not pose as serious a problem for physicians as patients who lack secondary education. This latter group of patients make the practice of shared understanding especially difficult to bring about. This is because they can't process the information adequately or understand what is being disclosed. This adds to the difficulty of treating such patients because being clear and concise isn't helpful. They pose special problems that are beyond the scope of this book.

b. Differing levels of patient reflectiveness and comprehension could also affect a patient's understanding of the alternatives disclosed. It is easy for a physician to determine whether a terminally-ill patient is sufficiently reflective so that (s)he will not make hasty decisions about medical treatments. Reflective patients usually insist on having an adequate amount of time to think about the treatments, ask questions about important aspects of the treatment and their illness that they don't understand, and decide whether to start a treatment based on their values, goals, and life plans. If the patient asks such questions, she is reflective.

Although most patients seem to be sufficiently reflective, except perhaps for the uneducated, the quality and degree of a patient's reflective capacity may still vary substantially. Some patients may be reflective enough to think about the treatments disclosed by the physician, but may still decide to undergo a treatment hastily, not taking the necessary time to carefully reflect on the treatments and their side effects. Some of these patients usually fail to have a coherent set of values, goals, and life plans available for them to make a proper, autonomous choice about a medical treatment. Yet other patients are quite unreflective. In this case, the physician must ***guide*** an unreflective patient's thinking in an unbiased manner such that (s)he can make a proper decision for or against treatment.

c. Three psychological factors can influence a patient's understanding. These are: (i) relentless pain and fatigue; (ii) feelings of hopelessness and depression; and (iii) denial.

   i. **Relentless pain and fatigue** can affect a terminally-ill patient's capacity to understand the information about the treatments disclosed by the physician. When a terminally-ill patient is in constant pain, (s)he may not be able to concentrate properly. The terminally-ill patient usually desires to have his/her pain lessened as soon as possible. Therefore, such patients may 'frame' treatment solutions hastily because of their pain and discomfort levels. Upon recognition of such difficulties, physicians should take steps to *guide* a terminally-ill patient's thinking so that (s)he chooses the most appropriate treatments. In this way, the patient may be able to *step back* from his/her pain for a short time and make a decision that is based on an objective understanding of all the treatments available.

ii. **Feelings of hopelessness and depression** may also be detrimental to a terminally-ill patient's capacity for understanding the treatments since such feelings can irrationally sway the patient towards inappropriate treatments. A terminally-ill patient does not have a *normal* life. Life is a constant uphill battle with no rhyme or reason sometimes. This can make rational unbiased decisions difficult to bring about.

Terminally-ill patients will *frame* the treatments differently from an acutely-ill patient. Acutely ill patients undergo treatment, take time to recover, and then resume their normal lives. However, a terminally-ill patient's reality is very different. The long-term nature of the illness may bias patients to *frame* decisions in terms of how hopeless they feel. The physician must keep this tendency towards biased decisions in mind since such decisions would be negative in nature.

iii. **Denial** is normal for a patient living with a terminal illness. Such patients are usually in denial about their illness and disability. Such an unrealistic mindset usually disrupts the mental composure of the patient. For some terminally-ill patients, the grief experienced is stronger and more intense than for other types of patients. This occurs for several reasons.

First, the terminally-ill patient may not have effective coping skills in place to deal with the symptoms of the fatigue and pain she experiences. Some patients may feel angry and depressed because of the continuous nature of pain and increased disability they experience. It may sometimes be necessary for the physician to recommend that the patient seeks counselling to learn how to best cope with the illness.

Second, the patient may not have a support system in place with people who are in a similar situation. Many families don't help terminally-ill patients and the unpredictable nature of the illness makes it especially difficult for the patient to be consistent with symptoms and fatigue levels. Family members may not believe the hardship the patient experiences because she *looks relatively healthy*. This can make terminally-ill patients feel even more alone and desperate at times. There's nothing worse than suffering in isolation. So, it is important for patients to seek support systems outside of the realm of their family. Contact your local chapter of the Arthritis Society or go online and seek out support groups. There are many opportunities out there; we just must seek them out.

Third, the patient may be experiencing a difficult time because (s)he never expected to become terminally-ill. Terminal illness can be overwhelming to live with at first. Thus, it is important for a patient to take time to come to terms with the idea that she can no longer do as much as she did before. Unless terminally-ill patients grieve properly, they will be bitter and enraged as time goes on.

By taking these three psychological factors that can influence shared understanding into consideration, physicians can ensure that their patients have effectively understood the potential treatments. Without an understanding of the treatments, patients cannot make a rational decision about the treatment which is best for them.

Terminally-ill patients offer new challenges for the physician, some of which may be difficult to overcome, given a physician's time constraints. There are no easy solutions for physicians. The difficulty is exacerbated by patients who can't psychologically come to terms with their illness. By trying to ensure that patients understand their treatment options, physicians come closer to advocating patient-centered care, and when it comes to terminal care, that is very laudable indeed.

CHAPTER 6

Rational Decision-Making

In this chapter, I will discuss rational decision making, the third condition of the patient-centered approach for the terminally-ill patient. Rational decision-making is important since patients who suddenly become terminally-ill may not be able to make rational decisions about future medical treatments on their own.

It is, therefore, essential that the terminally-ill patient make his/her decisions about treatment in conjunction with the physician. This is because a patient's decision-making capabilities may be biased due to the initial shock of hearing a negative diagnosis. The physician's role is to *guide* the patient to make a rational decision about future medical treatments.

Some patients may be in denial about their dire medical situation. Everyone wants to believe that they will always be alive and healthy. However, when we become terminally-ill this is an illusion since most of us will ultimately suffer from some terminal illness at some point in our lives and we will have to make some important choices about treatment and how we will live the rest of our lives.

Other patients may opt out of treatment altogether. This is understandable and is an option, given their terminal illness. However, the decision must be made in a rational and unbiased manner. Also, the decision must be derived through an informed consent. Then the patient can decide to live without treatment or medical interventions until his/her natural end.

In this chapter, I will focus on several overarching aspects of rational decision-making which underlie the patient-centered approach to medicine at the end-of-life.

PRELIMINARY CHARACTERIZATIONS

For the purposes of this discussion, a successful decision is a rational choice that a patient makes which is consistent with his/her values, goals, beliefs and life plans, and one which is not influenced by biases and prejudices which are irrelevant to the decision at hand.

It is essential, therefore, for physicians to *guide* a patient's decisions, especially when end-of-life choices must be made. For instance, if a terminally-ill patient is on medication, in constant pain, or experiencing fatigue, this may further undermine his/her ability to think rationally. Some terminally-ill patients may even bias their remaining years of life with a fatalist view of their life, and not seeing it as the true gift that it is.

For instance, many times patients who receive a dire, life-altering diagnosis could live for decades afterwards. These are patients who decided to defy the odds when they were diagnosed and accepted treatments and surgical interventions. They did not view their disease as the end-of-life and bias their decision against treatment because of these confirmation biases. Instead, they chose to be hopeful.

Further, biased thinking can lead to many errors of judgement. A biased decision is defined as a one-sided decision, lacking a neutral viewpoint or an open mind. Therefore, its essential for patients to make a rational decision in favor or against treatment.

This third condition of the patient-centered approach is much more complex than the first two conditions since a physician may have to guide the terminally-ill patient's decision by unintentionally projecting some of his/her values, outcomes and conclusions onto the patient's decision making in a way that may seem paternalistic.

According to the patient-centered model, any paternalistic decision-making is not permissible since it violates a patient's capacity of making his/her own rational and autonomous decisions about medical treatments. Physicians must, therefore, ensure that they are *guiding* the terminally-ill patient but not *prescribing* what they consider to be the most beneficial treatments on the patient's behalf. To *guide* means to *think along with* 'the terminally-ill patient, helping him/her to deliberate rationally and reflectively. This process is typically most effective when physicians keep asking the terminally-ill patient relevant questions about the treatments and possible surgical procedures to ensure that (s)he has, in fact, fully understood them at each point of disclosure.

DIMENSIONS OF RATIONAL DECISION MAKING

Patients who are terminally-ill usually experience pain and disability for a prolonged time. Such patients have often been prescribed mind-altering and debilitating medications. Therefore, the physician must devise special methodologies and procedures for making medical decisions alongside such a patient. These procedures are usually unique to each patient.

It is obvious that physicians cannot ensure that a rational decision is made by each terminally-ill patient; however, if a patient has substantial self-knowledge, then the difficulty is manageable, and an informed consent about a treatment could still be achieved. Rational decisions cannot usually be made by terminally-ill patients who lack any kind of self-knowledge.

Therefore, there are three dimensions of rational decision-making:

1. Reflective deliberation;
2. Reflective Awareness; and
3. Empathic understanding.

I will examine each of the three dimensions of rational decision-making below.

I. REFLECTIVE DELIBERATION

The successful achievement of reflective deliberation presupposes that the terminally-ill patient has rationally evaluated his/her choice of treatments. To rationally deliberate about a treatment, a patient must not allow emotional and/or psychological influences to enter with their decision-making process.

This is a difficult stage of the deliberative process since when a patient is living with a terminal illness, (s)he feels vulnerable because of the continuous pain and other kinds of distresses such as end-of-life planning, funeral arrangements, talking to family to break the news about their disease, and so on. But this is precisely what biasing your decision means. Instead of planning death, patients should be planning the rest of their lives. The latter mindset can help patients have a better quality of life.

There are ways that physicians can guide terminally-ill patients to be more reflective by ensuring that biases in decision making do not occur. It can take a lot of patience for the physician to ensure that the terminally-ill patient makes a rational decision. This is one of most important tasks that a physician must achieve since without rational reflection, terminally-ill patients will fail to give an informed consent for or against treatment. And, therefore, their decision making will be irrational.

2. REFLECTIVE AWARENESS

Reflective awareness is a process through which the mind becomes aware of its own operations. A more practical characterization of reflective awareness is that it is a process of examining our thinking processes, trying to determine how we derived our initial assessments. To achieve this, a terminally-ill patient must become introspective about his/her own thinking processes and retrace his/her initial deliberations.

The terms 'introspective', 'reflective', and 'deliberative' have distinctive meanings and should not be conflated or considered to mean the same thing. In introspection, an individual must become aware of his/her own thinking processes that make up those deliberative processes. Introspection is a process that makes it possible to become aware of ordinary deliberation and reflective awareness. The evaluative stage of awareness occurs at the reflective stage when the patient makes a judgement about the thinking processes.

Reflective awareness substantially increases a terminally-ill patient's chances of making a rational decision about a medical treatment. It ensures that the patient will take the time to critically evaluate all the medical information disclosed by the physician and ensure that this decision is consistent with his/her values, beliefs, and remaining life goals. This evaluative analysis takes a considerable amount of time to achieve and depends on the terminally-ill patient's ability to reflect. Different individuals have different capacities for this type of complex reflection, and not every person is equally reflective. For individuals who are psychologically debilitated by continuous pain, fatigue and medication, the reflective process must be repeated a few times to determine whether their initial evaluations were accurate.

Thus, reflective awareness signifies more than the freedom to choose between alternative modes of medical treatment. It requires that a terminally ill patient makes a reflective choice that represents his/her deeply held beliefs and preferences and not merely those of a brief or fleeting duration. In other words, the patient must seek out those beliefs that are permanent and stable parts of his/her self. Terminally-ill patients are more than a bundle of individual behaviours;

they are capable of reflective awareness which ensures careful reflection of their decisions.

When reflective awareness is effective, the physician will not be subject to nearly as much uncertainty in obtaining a rational decision in favour of a medical procedure. It will be possible to be much more confident in determining whether the terminally-ill patient has adequately understood the information disclosed, and whether his/her decision was influenced by other irrelevant considerations.

The physician can do this by being attentive to the kinds of questions that the terminally-ill patient asks and the clarifications that (s)he believes are critical to his/her making a proper decision. Most terminally-ill patients will make decisions that are consistent with the type of individuals they are. This will help the physician most accurately determine which patients need to be guided to make an effective medical decision and which ones can make decisions on their own. Typically, if a patient exhibits reflective awareness, (s)he can make rational decisions in favour of a treatment. However, for patients who are not sufficiently reflective, they will need guidance from the physician.

What should a physician do if, while disclosing the information about a medical treatment, (s)he recognizes that the patient cannot engage in effective reflective deliberation and will inevitably make his/her decision in an unreflective manner? Does the physician have a duty to probe further to ensure the terminally-ill patient comprehends all the information presented in a reflective manner?

On the patient-centered approach, reflective deliberation is a central requirement of rational decision-making and of an informed consent; therefore, the physician has a duty to ensure that a patient's decision is autonomous and calculative in nature. The physician can help the patient further reflect by encouraging him or her to a more rational reflection. Some medical practitioners may believe that this is placing an unwarranted burden on the physician. I beg to differ on this point. Instead, I believe it is the physician's prerogative to make certain that the patient's decisions are as rational as possible. But while most terminally-ill patients can make rational decisions to some degree, some patients need a lot more guidance than others to make rational and reflective decisions about medical treatments.

3. EMPATHIC UNDERSTANDING

Another important feature of patient-centered health care is for the physician to ensure that the patient gives a rational consent in favour or against treatment. From a personal perspective, the terminally-ill patient may be depressed about his/her illness and in constant pain. Empathy can help a physician detect many forms of psychological distress.

If a patient's psychological distress goes untreated, it can cause that patient to become prematurely despondent about his/her terminal condition. Thus, it is important for the physician to sufficiently get to know the terminally-ill patient to determine whether different aspects of his/her terminal condition should be treated before (s)he decides in favour of treatment.

This is the interpersonal component of obtaining an informed consent for treatment. Through an empathic understanding of the terminally-ill patient's situation and by developing a relationship of mutual trust and respect, the physician will be able to determine whether (s)he should help the patient choose the best treatment option. Below, I outline four guidelines that physicians could try to ensure that a terminally-ill patient gives an informed consent for treatment.

First, a physician must gain a sufficient amount of knowledge about the patient, not only in terms of his/her medical history but how (s)he is uniquely coping with his/her terminal condition. This process involves becoming aware of the patient's beliefs, values, desires, long and short-term goals, principles, moral and/or religious inclinations. In addition, it is essential that the physician gain a sufficient amount of information about the patient's temperament, character traits, and attitudes.

For instance, the physician should know whether the patient is predominantly happy, unhappy, sad, and in a happy or unhappy marriage, and so on. Such psychological factors can have a negative impact on the patient's overall health and outlook. This is especially the case when the patient becomes terminally-ill since such an individual will usually develops a cynical attitude towards him/herself and will become increasingly prone to experiencing even more negative emotions.

Thus, through an empathic understanding of the patient's attitudes before the onset of the terminal illness, the physician can be aware of the patient's attitudes. The more the physician strives to gain an empathic understanding of the patient's unique situation, the more empathic can the physician become with the patient's medical situation.

Second, the decision in favour of a treatment must be made by the patient in collaboration with the physician. Ideally, the terminally-ill patient should always openly communicate his/her medical needs to the physician. It is essential that the physician become reflexively aware of the patient's medical concerns and any familial idiosyncrasies, such as whether there is a manipulative spouse, financial difficulties, and so on. Stress can wreak havoc with a terminally-ill patient's ability to cope with the illness. Therefore, this kind of empathic interaction can help the patient better cope with the symptoms.

Third, the patient's request for treatment must be continuous, conscious, reflective and freely made. There is so much room for abuse in this area that it is essential for a physician to empathically communicate directly with the terminally-ill patient. This will ensure that the patient decides which is informed and unbiased. If a patient feels pressured, (s)he should step back for a while before deciding. In this way, the physician could empathically respond to the patient's needs. However, if the patient makes continuous and consistent requests in favour of a treatment, and these requests are rational, and the decision doesn't appear to be biased, then his/her request in favour of or against a treatment will be genuine.

Fourth, the physician must empathically determine whether the patient's pain and suffering can be relieved by other means. Sometimes, there are other medical treatments available to a patient. For example, a terminally-ill patient's illness may not be progressing as quickly as initially anticipated. Therefore, the patient may not need to undergo aggressive treatments and prescribing more pain medication may be the answer. It is important for the physician to be empathic with the patient's terminal illness, pain, and suffering by imagining what it would be like to be in the patient's predicament. In other words, the physician must ask him/herself: *How would I feel if I had this terminal condition?* This will give the physician an idea of how the patient may be feeling.

Rational decision-making is especially important for the terminally-ill patient who must decide about treatment. Many times, patients may make decisions in favour of or against treatments which are counterintuitive and biased. Thus, the physician should always determine if the patient should be *guided* to successfully make rational decisions. This does not mean that the physician must decide on the patient's behalf. The physician's role is merely one of *guiding* the patient's thinking processes so that (s)he could make a rational decision that is free from biases. Thus, the physician merely plays the role of collaborator of decision-making. Some physicians still resist shared decision-making because of the psychological complexity that is involved in such situations. However, shared decision-making can sometimes save a patient's undue hardship and ensure that (s)he is making a rational decision about future interventions.

Thus, physicians may need to spend a substantial amount of time guiding some of their patients' thinking processes. Some terminally-ill patients may lack the kind of reflective awareness that is necessary to make assessments about previously made decisions. The physician should not expect the patient to proceed on his/her own since, given the medical situation, that patient may lack the kind of objective reflection that is necessary to make a rational decision.

This process requires that the physician and patient engage in effective communication to reach a rational decision about a medical treatment together. Effective communication, in turn, requires that an open, honest physician-patient relationship is developed by the physician. I turn to this topic in the next chapter.

CHAPTER 7

Developing an Effective Physician-Patient Relationship

The fourth condition of a patient-centered approach is for the physician to take steps to develop and nurture an effective physician-patient relationship. To develop this condition, the physician must have a knowledge of the terminally-ill patient's beliefs, values, and life goals. Every terminally-patient will have different needs for information-disclosure about his/her condition, depending on personal idiosyncrasies. Unless the physician is aware of these personal differences in advance, (s)he will be unable to disclose the relevant information about treatments to the patient.

Open and honest communication is difficult to develop and maintain if the physician doesn't disclose all the details of the treatment to the patient. To develop an effective physician-patient relationship, the patient must trust that the physician has disclosed all the information about the available treatments. In addition, the physician must trust that the patient has understood all the treatment options. This reciprocal relationship of trust is one of the building blocks of an effective physician-patient relationship.

There are two central features of an effective physician-patient relationship: effective disclosure, and shared decision-making between physician and patient. In Part I, I will focus on the first feature of an effective physician-patient relationship, while in Part II I will concentrate on the second.

The unacceptable practise of using manipulative techniques to communicate the medical alternatives to the terminally-ill patient will be considered in Part I since shared decision making it impossible without honest, open, non-manipulative communication between the patient and physician. A physician who makes use of manipulative techniques to convince the patient to undergo a treatment minimizes any chance of developing an effective physician-patient relationship.

DISCLOSURE WITHOUT MANIPULATION

On the patient-centered approach, any exchange between physician and patient must be free from manipulative techniques. Such techniques may lead to forced decisions that are not informed. Rather, the treatments must be disclosed to the terminally-ill patient free from psychological manipulations and in such a way as to consider the patient's beliefs, values, and life goals. There are four kinds of manipulations that can be used by physicians: (1) Coercion; (2) Persuasion; (3)

Prematurely prioritizing the information presented; (4) Tone of Voice.

(1) Coercion is defined as the intentional influences that pose or exaggerate a credible threat of unwanted and avoidable harm, so influential that the terminally-ill patient cannot resist acting to avoid it. In such a case, the terminally-ill patient would be consenting to treatment that is not necessarily in his/her best interest, and hence the decision made would be uninformed.

This occurs most notably when the physician is dogmatically convinced that the patient should undergo a medical intervention without recognizing the patient's values and needs at the time. If the terminally-ill patient unreflectively submits to the physician's coercions and accepts a treatment that she hasn't decided upon him/herself, (s)he will not necessarily agree with the physician's recommendation but may still accept it to avoid being a nuisance.

Very few physicians use coercive techniques due to peer pressure and the irrational response that it tends to produce in the patient. Physicians usually use coercion only as a last resort if they believe that the patient is refusing treatment that (s)he should at least try out. For instance, if a physician believes that a terminally-ill patient should undergo an elective surgery that may help him/her better cope with the disease, the physician may try to convince the patient by saying: *If you don't have surgery, you'll only live a few months*. This tactic can also be used to convince a patient to undergo surgery as the quickest way to alleviate complications with the illness.

In other words, by undergoing surgery, the terminally-ill patient may gain more freedom from devastating pain and symptoms and prolong her life at least in the short-term. However, even if a terminally-ill patient makes an irrational decision against surgery, the physician should resist using coercive techniques to convince him/her to undergo surgery.

Instead, the physician should guide the terminally-ill patient's thinking so that (s)he will eventually make a more rational decision the second or third time the information about the treatments is presented. Some patients make decisions in favour of certain treatments that are initially irrational, yet upon the second and third reassessment of the treatment alternatives, such patients become convinced that their previous decision was irrational.

Some patients may have had family members or close friends who had bad experiences undergoing certain surgeries or treatments. This may lead these patients to think they will have the same kind of fate themselves. But this kind of biased thinking can lead to erroneous consent in favor or against a treatment or procedure.

(2) Persuasion may be characterized as the successful attempt by the physician to convince a terminally-ill patient, through appeals to reason or emotion, in favour of a treatment that the physician believes (s)he should undergo to improve his/her overall health and well-being. When a terminally-ill patient's beliefs are manipulated by the physician, (s)he is persuaded to undergo a medical treatment that may not be in accordance with the values of that patient. This is the most problematic of the two types of manipulation since it is sometimes difficult for a terminally-ill patient to correctly ascertain whether (s)he is being persuasively influenced by the physician. Sometimes, the physician persuades the patient so subtly that (s)he is even unaware of being persuaded.

Therefore, the patient is unaware of whether his/her decision in favour of a treatment was informed or uninformed.

(3) Terminally-ill patients may sometimes be influenced by the order in which the medical treatments are presented since they may believe that the information that the physician presents first must be the most beneficial for them. Ideally, the treatments should be ordered by both the physician and patient. By ordering the treatments without the patient's consent, the physician may be manipulating the patient by presenting the most viable treatment option first so that the patient will remember it before (s)he reaches his/her cognitive saturation point.

(4) If a physician speaks in a loud or abrupt tone of voice, this may give the terminally-ill patient a feeling of uneasiness. This feeling may then carry over and the patient may feel obligated to agree to a procedure without giving an informed consent. This may again result in the patient accepting a treatment unconsciously.

Soft voices, on the other hand, may connote acceptance and less risk. Terminally-ill patients interpret such verbal cues in a variety of non-rational ways, depending on their state of vulnerability. Therefore, a loud tone of voice can be a manipulative technique that must be avoided by the physician.

On the patient-centered approach, it is never acceptable for physicians to use any of the above manipulative techniques to convince terminally-ill patients to decide in favour of a medical procedure the physician believes is the most appropriate. This is because such a condescending attitude undermines a patient's autonomy and the physician-patient relationship.

Such manipulative techniques can also reinforce the paternalistic model of medicine which states that the physician is the authority over the patient's treatment. No consent is needed on this model since the physician assumes that (s)he knows what is in the patient's best interest. Consent under the traditional model focuses on harm-avoidance above all else, even if it means undermining a patient's autonomy. On the patient-centered model, all consent given by a terminally-ill patient must be autonomous. Thus, it is never appropriate for the physician to undermine the patient's basic right to give an informed consent for a treatment.

There are several known reasons why physicians feel justified in using manipulative techniques when treating terminally-ill patients. These are: (i) Time constraints; (ii) Deficiency in a patient's psychological competency; (iii) Lack of physician patience; (iv) The patient's failure to understand medical terminology.

However, each of these justifications can coerce patients into medical decisions which undermine a patient's right to making an informed decision for him/herself. Thus, on the patient-centered model, these rationalizations must be avoided by the physician. Because they are so common, it is important to examine each of them in detail to understand why some physicians may still feel the necessity of using them.

i. There is no doubt that physicians are overworked and overstressed due to the everyday pressures inherent in medical practise. Despite this, a physician is never justified in undermining a patient's basic right to make an informed decision for him/herself, except in justified emergency situations. Thus, the time constraints that a physician faces are not usually an insurmountable obstacle to developing an effective physician-patient relationship.

ii. Every terminally-ill patient has a different level of psychological competence and emotional intelligence. The physician should try to become aware of the terminally-ill patient's unique level of reflection and awareness before disclosing information about the treatments.

Most terminally-ill patients are psychologically competent to make their own decisions about a medical treatment. Some terminally-ill patients should be *guided* by the physician into making an autonomous decision about a medical treatment. Under no circumstances is it permissible for the physician to be manipulative or coercive. However, the physician has a duty to ensure that the patient's decision in favour of a treatment is rational and reflective.

iii. Physicians must allow a sufficient amount of time to disclose all the relevant treatments, and the risks and benefits involved. Disclosure of information is typically a time-consuming process, but the physician has a duty to ensure that (s)he spends as much time as is necessary for a patient to understand all the information relayed. The time required will vary from patient to patient. For some patients, the physician may need to schedule several sessions to disclose the information.

iv. Some physicians believe that they have expert knowledge that cannot possibly be understood by the typical patient. This is a faulty assumption since every profession has its own technical jargon which most lay persons can understand, given all the ways they could attain such information, through the internet and learning channels on television.

All technical terms have an explanation in ordinary language that can be easily understood. Thus, physicians should carefully use nontechnical language when communicating the treatments available to the patient. Failure to do so may be construed as a form of manipulation since it undermines a patient's right to understand the treatments available to him/her.

Building an effective physician-patient relationship is based on developing openness and trust. This is best achieved by clearly and openly communicating with a patient. However, given the sensitive nature of the disclosures and communications between the patient and physician, it is essential for both parties to develop an effective relationship. This can be hard to achieve but it is worth it for patients in the last stages of life.

CHAPTER 8

Shared Decision Making

The fifth condition of the patient-centered approach is shared decision making which encourages the equal distribution of decision making between the physician and patient. Most simply defined, the physician's role is to use his/her training, knowledge, and expertise to provide the patient with facts about the diagnosis and prognosis with or without treatments.

Then, the patient's role is to use her values and goals to evaluate the possible treatments, and to select one that she feels is best. However, this ideal has many challenges. The facts/values division of labour is hard to bring about in every medical situation. However, within the patient-centered approach, it is necessary for physicians to try to achieve shared decision making with their patients. Patients want to be consulted about the impact of their treatments at every juncture.

Shared decision making consists of: (1) acknowledging uncertainty; (2) sharing authority; (3) developing mutual trust and respect; and (4) respecting a patient's autonomy. Shared decision making can be difficult for some medical professionals to accept because of the paternalistic tradition that has been in effect in medicine for a long time. Traditionally, medicine has been viewed by the public as a stable and reliable profession.

When a terminally-ill patient needs medical education, it is now common for him/her to believe that the science of medicine will usually help him/her by lessening pain and discomfort. The terminally-ill patient may even get better and have less pain and fatigue in time. There has been a concern by medical professionals that shared decision making between the patient and physician may result in a public awareness of some of the known uncertainties inherent in end-of-life care. Some physicians may feel that, if the terminally-ill patient becomes aware of these uncertainties, (s)he may feel even more vulnerable and uncertain. This isn't usually the case, however. Most patients want to know the facts about their terminal illness and the prognosis.

(1) Shared decision making sometimes involves the tension of uncertainty because physicians must not only disclose information about medical treatments, but they must also communicate any uncertainties about a medical treatment to the patient. This involves giving the terminally-ill patient information about the probabilities of success for a medical treatment, in addition to the possibilities that the treatment may be unsuccessful. By becoming aware of the success rate

of a treatment, the patient can have the necessary information about the track record of a treatment to make an informed decision for or against treatment. Terminally-ill patients may still choose treatments that have low probabilities of success; however, they will be autonomously deciding in favour of a treatment, given its success rate for other patients.

(2) Physicians may sometimes find it difficult to disclose uncertainties to their terminally-ill patients since medicine is usually considered to be stable and reliable. However, the unknown dimensions of terminal illness make medicine for the patient somewhat unpredictable and uncertain. Unfortunately, this is part of being terminally-ill. Some physicians would prefer to keep this uncertainty hidden from their patients since they want to uphold their professionalism and the trust that patients may have in them. But this is not the case any more, given the transparency of the medical profession because of social media.

(3) Sharing authority in decision-making does not necessarily mean that physicians and terminally-ill patients must make a joint decision about a medical treatment. What shared authority usually means is that the physician must *guide* the terminally-ill patient into making a nonbiased decision in favour of a medical intervention. This will ensure that the terminally-ill patient will make an autonomous decision for a medical treatment.

The main goal of shared decision-making is for the physician to ensure that the terminally-ill patient makes a substantially autonomous decision about a treatment. However, if the physician and patient do not form a partnership-type relationship in which each person equally contributes to the decision-making process, an autonomous, rational, and reflective decision about a medical treatment is difficult, if not impossible, to achieve.

Therefore, shared decision making consists of developing a mutual dependency relationship between the patient and physician. The physician cannot disclose the information about medical alternatives without some personal knowledge of the patient, and the patient cannot decide without an adequate disclosure of medical information. Both the terminally-ill patient and physician are authorities in different ways, in that the patient is an authority on his/her personal goals, values and beliefs, while the physician has the medical knowledge to help the terminally-ill patient. Thus, shared authority is an essential feature of an effective physician-patient relationship.

The old, traditional paternalistic model of the physician as a prescriber of medications and treatments has been dethroned. It has become a physician's implicit responsibility to ensure and assist the terminally-ill patient to make autonomous, rational, and reflective decisions about his/her medical treatments. This requires that terminally-ill patients make their own decisions about the medical treatments that will affect the rest of their lives. In other words, patients must determine for themselves which medical procedures and treatments they will physically endure. On the patient-centered approach, this is required to respect a terminally-ill patient's autonomy.

For shared decision making, the terminally-ill patient and physician must trust one another. An effective physician-patient relationship is built on trust. Due to the vulnerabilities of the medical profession's uncertainties and the patient's illness, mutual trust is essential to foster a relationship where the two parties can achieve open, honest communication.

Mutual trust has two dimensions, one for the physician and one of the terminally-ill patients. The patient must trust that the physician will disclose all the information honestly and openly to ensure that (s)he can reach a rational decision in favour of a medical treatment. The physician must, in turn, trust that the patient will understand and use all the information competently to make a rational and autonomous decision about treatment.

When I say that the physician must trust the patient, I mean that (s)he trusts that the patient has reflected sufficiently on all the relevant aspects of the treatments. This presupposes that the terminally-ill patient has understood all the information relayed and (s)he has communicated all his/her questions to the physician in order that they may be rectified. This trust may take the form of an intuition on the part of the physician about his/her terminally-ill patient.

Building mutual trust and respect between patient and physician is an essential condition for establishing a healthy physician-patient relationship. It takes a substantial amount of time, effort, and maturity on the part of both the physician and patient to develop such a trusting relationship. Trust is built on more than actions alone.

Effective communication between physician and patient is also required to achieve an informed consent. The trust that is developed between the physician and patient requires more than the mere trust that (s)he has that his/her physician has the medical expertise to perform the treatment adequately. In addition, physicians should not hesitate to share their difficulties in decision making with their patients.

However, trust and respect between the terminally-ill patient and physician are not easily acquired virtues. Physicians must strive to give both a diseased body and a diseased person its proper importance and where conflicts arise, they must reconcile whether they will give preference to the diseased body or diseased person.

Within the patient-centered approach, a diseased patient takes precedence over the diseased body since the patient makes an autonomous decision in favour of a treatment. There is no necessary boundary between the body and the person since whatever happens to the body always influences the person and the person usually deals with the illness. Thus, the physician must focus on both the physical and psychological dimensions of the patient.

(4) The physician must respect a patient's autonomy by cultivating an effective relationship in which the patient is given ample time and space to make his/her own decision about a medical treatment. Within the traditional, paternalistic model, patients were viewed as vulnerable children instead of autonomous adults. Terminal illness may weaken a patient's ability to make autonomous decisions; however, it doesn't undermine their ability altogether. A patient who is terminally-ill can still make rational decisions although the process of decision making may take considerably longer. But this is part of the challenge of treating terminally-ill patients.

There are times that a physician may impatiently frame a terminally-ill patient as being incapable of rational decision-making, and thus proceed to either use some form of manipulative approach to prescribe a treatment. Unless there is a good reason to assume that a patient completely lacks a sense of what (s)he wants, the physician must always assume that the patient can make autonomous decisions on his/her own. Anything less may result in erroneously undermining patient autonomy which is not instrumental to developing an effective physician-patient relationship.

In this chapter, I discussed the importance of developing an effective physician-patient relationship so that shared decision making is possible. One of the chief features of developing such a relationship is to effectively communicate and engage in shared decision-making. This presupposes the development of mutual trust and respect between physician and patient. A patient-centered approach cannot be developed without developing an effective physician-patient relationship. In the next chapter, I will discuss the unpredictable nature of terminal illness.

CHAPTER 9

Accepting the Unpredictable Nature of With End-of-Life Care

The nature of end-of-life care is unpredictable for both patients and physicians alike. It can be difficult for a terminally-ill patient to accurately assess how (s)he will feel over time. This is because terminal illness has no predictable progression.

Some patients with terminal illness may even become pain-free for a while. Others never experience an end to their pain and misery. Such patients usually come to their physician's office looking for help from their pain, and yet the physician can't do very much to help them. This is when the physician and patient can become frustrated.

In fact, much of the self-management must come from the patient, the person who feels weakened because of the constant pain and disability that (s)he experiences. Sadly, this is the fate that a terminally-ill patient lives through.

Some physicians may find treating terminally-ill patients frustrating and unsatisfying because they feel unable to cure the patient or give him/her a treatment with definitive results. Instead, the physician must encourage the patient to accept his/her situation and carry on in the best way possible.

Thus, most of a physician's consultation with a terminally-ill patient is dealing with the personal and psychological aspects of the illness. This requires that medical facts don't take as much precedence as the subjective components of the illness and the way in which the patient is coping with his/her illness from day-to-day. For physicians, this changes the medical encounter from an objective, fact-based assessment to a value-filled subjective assessment which has no clear-cut answers or treatments, making the medical encounter especially unpredictable and messy for the physician treating terminally-ill patients.

Most patients hate being in pain, and they especially hate being in constant pain. Most physician visits by a terminally-ill patient center on pain and further decline. Patients want relief from the constant grind of pain and the hardship and fatigue that is associated with it.

Yet, physicians and specialists have no idea what to do about the pain either than prescribing pain medications and talking to the patient at length about how to manage his/her life differently. Each patient will struggle with pain and physical decline very differently because the experience of pain is patient-specific. Some patients have a low pain threshold while others have a high one. This can make the physician's job of treating a terminal pain complex and multi-faceted.

In this chapter, I will offer a few tips on how physicians can help the patient with the unique symptoms of his/her disease.

In Chapter 1, I outlined what patients can do to help themselves with their terminal condition. In this chapter, I focused on what the physician can do to help the patient. There are many things that physicians could suggest that terminally-ill patients try, depending on how open and receptive a patient is to help him/herself with the pain. Some terminally-ill patients will want to do anything they can to help themselves. Other patients will be more sceptical and won't be open to helping themselves out at all. Neither will they want to do things that are proactive for their health and well-being. If a patient isn't open to improving his/her life, there's nothing that a physician can do to help the patient. In such cases, the physician just must leave the patient to his own devices.

There are a few things that physicians could suggest to receptive patients.

First, physicians can encourage patients to take control of the symptoms of their illness and not be paralyzed by them. This means that patients should try to live with the pain and fatigue of the terminal illness by moulding their lives to their terminal condition. Patients may have to pace themselves more and revise how they do their normal daily chores. For instance, terminally-ill patients may not be able to clean the whole house at one time.

Instead, they may only be able to spend ten or fifteen minutes vacuuming and then they'll have to sit down and rest. It may be difficult for terminally-ill patients to do this at first, but their overall well-being and quality of life depends on it. Terminally-ill patients must realize that their lives will never be the same as they were before the onset of their terminal illness. This is usually the hardest thing for patients to come to terms with.

It's the unpredictable nature of pain and the physical decline that unravels terminally-ill patients and physicians alike. Life feels like an uphill battle when a patient lives in constant pain. Some patients expect the pain to get worse all the time. This can make the patient feel that his/her pain is out of control. This can sometimes result from a misperception by the patient.

When a patient keeps framing the severity of the pain and decline prematurely, the patient won't be able to effectively cope with the disease because of the negative biasing. The only thing that a physician can be do in such a situation is to help the patient understand that (s)he has no control over the disease and must accept the disease and be as positive as possible and try to enjoy his/her remaining days.

Second, a patient's illness will not always be out of control. There will be times when the patient's pain will be more controlled. At such times, the patient will feel more able to cope with the illness. And this can really help the patient do some of the things that (s)he couldn't, given his/her pain and fatigue levels. It is important for patients not to give up hope.

So many patients who are in constant pain feel that life is an uphill battle. So many times, terminally-ill patients feel unable to cope with their illness which makes terminally-ill patients feel even more miserable. This negative feeling can hinder how a patient feels about him/herself and her life overall.

Thus, physicians should help patients develop a positive attitude. It is important for a patient to be able to effectively cope with a terminal illness. A terminally-ill patient can develop a positive attitude by living more in the present and not worrying about the future. Therefore, terminally-ill patients should try to live their lives to the fullest and not concern themselves about things that they cannot control.

In addition, terminally-ill patients should try not to develop a gloomy attitude towards their predicament because of their constant pain and fatigue. Even the simplest tasks are difficult for terminally-ill patients to perform on a bad day. So, keeping positive is crucially important. A physician could help the patient maintain a positive attitude by encouraging the patient and telling him/her not to ever give up.

Third, a physician can help the patient by encouraging him/her to develop an exercise regimen. There is nothing that will help a patient with a terminal illness more than exercise. However, it must be the correct exercise in the right amount. A patient shouldn't overdo such exertions.

Instead, the patient should start an exercise regimen slowly and build activity into his/her lives in small increments. Only then can the patient reap the benefits of exercise. When a terminally-ill patient exercises, (s)he releases feel good endorphins which makes him/her feel more confident and happy. This is very important for a terminally-ill patient who is struggling daily with a lot of pain and discomfort. Thus, terminally-ill patients need to be encouraged to start an exercise program and stick to it.

Fourth, a physician can send the patient for physiotherapy. Many times, physiotherapy can help with a patient's pain and discomfort. Most physicians know one or two good physiotherapists in their area who can help terminally-ill patients to increase range of motion and mobility. Also, the physiotherapist can apply heat and cold to the area to lessen pain and inflammation.

Further, physiotherapists can demonstrate some flexibility and strengthening exercises so that the terminally-ill patient will feel an increase in his/her mobility. The more flexible a terminally-ill patient becomes, the more in control of his/her disability will (s)he be. This can help the patient to feel better about his/her terminal condition.

Fifth, the physician could suggest that the patient go to a massage therapist. Many times, massage therapy can help a patient relax and improve how (s)he feels overall as well. Message can also help improve a patient's circulation. This can tremendously help a terminally-ill patient feel less pain and a lot more control. Massage therapists have a healing touch. They can help to relax and soothe the terminally-ill patient so that (s)he can feel the difference between a relaxed muscle and a tense one. A tense muscle can cause the patient a lot of pain while a relaxed one can help him/her feel more relaxed.

Sixth, the physician could suggest that the patient go to a counsellor if (s)he feels that such a patient is experiencing depression. Some terminally-ill patients become depressed. This can cause the patient to feel out of control and pessimistic about the future. If this negative feeling continues, the patient will start feeling down and perhaps even depressed. Also, if the patient is experiencing depression, (s)he will need a lot of unconditional love and care. Counsellors can help the patient put coping strategies in place so that their quality of life will improve.

Lastly, the physician should strive to treat the whole patient, not merely his/her illness. This is what it means to treat the patient in a humane manner. The best way to treat a terminally-ill patient is to treat the psychosocial aspects of the illness as much as the physical aspects. There's no point merely treating the physical aspects of the illness since for the terminally-ill patient, the mental components of the illness contribute just as much to the hardship of coping with the illness.

Thus, the patient should spend as much time talking about the psychological fears that the patient is experiencing as with the physical disabilities that the patient is experiencing. Terminal illness affects the whole patient. Therefore, the physician should also treat the whole patient as well to be successful.

The patient-centered approach advocated in this book is the best way to treat a terminally-ill patient. The terminally-ill patient requires a different kind of attention and care than acutely ill patients. Terminally-ill patients will come and may have to consult the physician for years about problems that have no clear-cut resolution.

Therefore, physicians need to treat terminally-ill patients in a very different manner. Many times, empathy and kindness can help more than prescribing medication. Other times, a friendly touch or a genuine concern can help the patient feel better. The patient-centered approach to treating the terminally-ill can be fulfilling for the physician too. All that is needed is a shift in attitude as well as a change in the ultimate goals of medicine from curing to caring.

Ideally, the patient-centered approach will help the patient feel more cared for and the physician more fulfilled. I hope this book helps the terminally-ill patient feel more in control of his/her illness and the physician to feel more able to help his/her patient. The terminally-ill patient poses challenges for the physician. The whole enterprise of medical practice must be rethought and stretched to accommodate the terminally-ill patient. However, if physicians adhere to the patient-centered approach, they should be able to treat terminally-ill patients in a humane manner, one that is fulfilling to them once and for all.

CHAPTER 10

A Humane Patient-Centered Approach to End-of-Life Care

The purpose of this chapter is to assess the patient-centered approach in terms of the three conditions outlined in Part II to achieve humane health care. As has been argued in the book thus far, the patient-centered approach is especially necessary for the terminally-ill patient since many times, the patient is unable to make an unbiased and rational decision in favour or against treatment. It is, therefore, essential that the physician ensure that the terminally-ill patient fulfill the three conditions of a patient-centered approach to health care outlined.

A terminally-ill patient can have two possible options. First, the patient can have surgery to alleviate some of the effects of the terminal illness. Alternatively, the patient can take different pain medications, including meds manage the negative effects of his/her illness. The physician can also recommend that the patient change his/her lifestyle to accommodate the terminal condition. The patient must learn to pace him/herself effectively, and not to overdo it. In either of these approaches, a patient must decide what to do, along with a specialist and/or medical practitioner.

The patient-centered approach is necessary to administer humane health care for the terminally-ill. Without personal and psychological information about the patient's values, the physician cannot ensure that a terminally-ill will give an informed consent for treatment. There are two foundational components of the patient-centered approach. First, the patient and physician should feel sufficiently comfortable with each other to openly and honestly discuss the patient's medical predicament. Second, the patient and physician should develop a partnership-type of relationship. Without developing this type of relationship, a terminally-ill patient's care will be less than effective.

THE COMPONENTS OF PATIENT-CENTERED APPROACH

Humane health care for the terminally-ill involves five components. Each of these components ensures that the patient's values and decisions are central components to the treatments proposed.

First, the physician must become sensitive to the patient's psychological needs and experience of illness. Terminally-ill patients have special needs that must be addressed if they are to feel that their quality of life is not substantially reduced.

Some patients may discover that they need to discuss their pain levels and fears about the future at length with the physician. Other patients have low pain thresholds, given their unique physiological and psychological make-up. The physician must determine the pain thresholds for each individual patient so that (s)he can prescribe proper medication to keep a patient as comfortable as possible.

Second, the physician must become aware of some of the qualitative features of the illness which will uniquely affect the patient's life. Terminal illness gravely affects a patient's life goals, and overall morale. It can also strain familial relationships and substantially restrict a patient's normal activities.

It is, therefore, essential for the physician to become aware of these restrictions so that (s)he can best help the patient recalibrate his/her life. Immediately after the diagnosis, the patient is unable to effectively cope with the symptoms of illness. Thus, the physician should encourage the patient to keep doing the activities which (s)he loves and enjoys for as long as possible. This will also help the patient better cope with his/her terminal condition.

Third, the physician must carefully listen to each patient's narrative of illness. Every terminally-ill patient has a life story to which his/her illness belongs. It is part of the patient-centered approach to allow these narratives to properly guide medical interventions.

For instance, the patient may have a stressful life having lived with an abusive spouse for a long time or may have been a smoker and overweight. These situations could negatively contribute to the patient's discomfort levels. It is extremely important for the physician to determine the patient's psychological and physical reasons for illness as much as possible. This will encourage the physician to determine how (s)he can best help the patient live the best life possible, given his/her illness.

Fourth, each terminally-ill patient will experience different emotions and feelings during his/her terminal illness. Some patients may become angry and depressed while others will insist on coping with the pain and hardship proactively. Thus, a physician must discuss the patient's feelings in relation to his/her terminal illness and any fears and future expectations that (s)he may have. If the physician detects that the patient is becoming depressed, (s)he should encourage the patient to see a counsellor. A counsellor could help encourage the patient to embrace the unknown aspects of his/her illness.

Fifth, the prognosis of every terminally-ill patient's illness must be assessed separately. Statistics may give the physician a better idea of the frequency of the terminal illness, given a patient's age group and life situation. However, each patient's life must be treated as intrinsically unique. A patient should never be compared to a statistic.

As each patient will experience the terminal illness differently, (s)he will endure the illness differently as well. Physicians should pay attention to the psychological aspects of the terminal illness since these aspects can become even more significant than the physical ones for terminally-ill patients over time.

CONCLUDING THOUGHTS

In this book, I have advocated the patient-centered approach to the terminally-ill patient in the last stages of life. This stage of life can be plagued with turmoil, hardship and devastation for the patient and family. The five conditions that I outlined in this book have highlighted some of the difficult aspects of administering health care to the terminally-ill patient. The five conditions have also showed that it can be very difficult to know how to treat a hopeless and devastated patient who is terminally-ill.

If successful, the five conditions of the patient-centered approach highlight some of the ways the patient should address his/her medical situation. It is never easy to receive a terminal diagnosis. It is time of great angst and shock, at least initially. However, if over time, the patient can come to terms and perhaps even accept his/her medical situation, the quality of such a patient's life can change for the better. And the better a patient feels about the situation, the better will his/her quality of life be.

Specialists and surgeons are usually very empathic with a terminally-ill patient's plight. There are also other levels of care that are open to the patient such as nurse practitioners, psychologists, counsellors, and physiotherapists. These people are there to chat with the patient and help him/her live the best possible life. The humane patient centered approach advocated here can also help remind the medical practitioners that there are many different levels to the patient's illness other than the physical/bodily disease. There are also all the psychological ramifications of the illness that must be dealt with in the most empathic way possible.

In this book, I have underlined the difficulty of a terminal diagnosis for both the patient and physician. It isn't easy to administer humane health care for a patient in the last stages of life. This is especially the case if the patient is despondent and doesn't really care about his/her life anymore. Such patients can find it hard to accept any treatment and most of their decisions against surgery and further treatments may be irrational. However, if the patient refuses treatment and surgery and makes the decision in a rational and informed way, what then?

The short answer is that if the patient decides that she doesn't want to live in agony and pain or doesn't want to undergo chemotherapy or other invasive treatments, then there is nothing that the physician can really do. It is kind of out of his hands. My focus has been to present an argument for what constitutes a good death for a patient and how the physician can best bring this about. Most of the onus of experiencing a good death is on the patient. If the patient decides that she doesn't want to live in agony and pain or doesn't want to undergo chemotherapy or other invasive treatments, then there is nothing that the physician can really do. It is kind of out of his hands.

The question that I would like to end this exploration on is how medical professionals can ensure that the terminally-ill patient has the best quality of life, given that (s)he is in the last stages of life. The five conditions of the patient-centered approach outlined in this book should help. However, ultimately patients must want to help themselves live the best last days that they can first and foremost. The physician can only do so much. If the patient keeps reiterating that (s)he doesn't want to do anything and just want to die naturally whenever the time comes (in agony, if necessary), then there is nothing that the physician or anyone else can do.

In other words, a good death can only be achieved by a patient if she has the will to do so. If a patient doesn't want to do anything than a good death cannot be achieved. To experience a good death takes a lot of work, energy and humility on the part of the patient. It is never easy to live our last stages of life with equanimity. But terminally-ill patients should try to do so to experience a good death.

We are blessed with a medical system here in Canada that has all the levels of care. And we are blessed that we have the best medical care system in the world when it comes to being taken care of medically and psychologically too. All we must do is to want to help ourselves and take concrete and realistic steps to have a good death.

It is easy to give up when a patient gets a serious diagnosis that is life threatening. It is one option that the patient has. However, a good death cannot arise unless the patient decides to be hopeful and to try to deify the odds of imminent death. Time and again, medical professionals have seen that terminally-ill patients can go into remission for a long time. This is because the patient decided to be hopeful, accept the medical situation that she is amid, and do the best she can to live the best possible life.

I believe that a patient can only experience a good death if she lives her last days hopefully and with the best quality of life possible. There is no surprise because if a person lives a meaningful life, regardless of whether she has received a life-altering diagnosis, and accepts all the treatments available, then she will live the best possible life. Then and only then can a patient experience a good death. Therefore, a good death is in the hands of the patient. We must be up to the challenge and willfully create a life that is meaningful. Are you up to the challenge?

Bibliography

Abu-Saad, Huda. *Evidence-Based Palliative Care: Across the Life Span.* Oxford: Blackwell Sciences Ltd., 2001.

Aring, Charles, D. "Sympathy and Empathy." *The Journal of the American Medical Association.* Volume 167(4), (1958), 448-452.

Barnard, David, Towers and Anna, Boston, Patricia, Lambrinidou, Yanna. *Crossing Over: Narratives of Palliative Care.* Oxford: Oxford University Press, 2000.

Beauchamp, T., & Childress, J. *Principles of Biomedical Ethics.* New York: Oxford University Press, 1979.

Bennett, Henry, L. "Trees and Heads: The Objective and the Subjective in Painful Procedures." *The Journal of Clinical Ethics,* 5(3), (1994), 149-151.

Bertakis, Klea, D., Roter, Debra, Putnam, Samuel, M. "The Relationship of Physician Medical Interview Style to Patient Satisfaction." *The Journal of Family Practice, 1991,* 32(2), 175-181.

Brody, Howard. *The Healer's Power.* New Haven and London: Yale University Press, 1987.

Brody, Howard. *Stories of Sickness*. New Haven and London: Yale University Press, 1992. Brody, Howard "Transparency: Informed Consent in Primary Care." *Hastings Center Report*. Volume 19 (1989), 5-9.

Brown, Dan. W. "Good Decision making for Incompetent Patients." *Special Supplement: Hastings Center Report*. November-December, (1994), S8-S10.

Buehler, David, A. "Informed Consent – Wishful Thinking?" *Journal of Medical and Human Bioethics*. Volume 4 (1982) 43-57.

Buller, Mary Klein, Buller David, B. "Physicians' Communication Style and Patient Satisfaction." *Journal of Health and Behavior*. Volume 28 (1987), 375-388.

Callanan, Maggie. *Final Journeys: A Practical Guide for Bringing Care and Comfort at the End-of-Life*. New York: Bantham Books, 2008.

Cassell, Eric. J. *The Healer's Art: A New Approach to the Doctor-Patient Relationship*. Philadelphia and New York: J.B. Lippincott Company, 1998.

Cassell, Eric. J. "The Function of Medicine." *The Hastings Center Report, (1977),* 16-19.

Coleman, Lester. L. "The Patient-Physician Relationship." *Physician's World*, 1974.

Dube, Laurette, Guylaine Ferland, D.S. Moskowitz. *Emotional & Interpersonal Dimensions of Health Services: Enriching the Art of Care with the Science of Care*. Montreal: McGill University Press, 2003.

Ehrenreich, Barbara. *Natural Causes: An Epidemic of Wellness, the Certainty of Dying, and Killing Ourselves to Live Longer.* New York: Hachette Book Group, 2018.

Elias, Sherman & Annas, George J. "The Whole Truth and Nothing but the Truth?" *Hastings Center Report,* Volume 18, (1988), 35-36.

Faden, Ruth, R. & Beauchamp, Tom L. *A History and Theory of Informed Consent.* New York: Oxford University Press, 1986.

Forrow, Lachlan. "The Green Eggs and Ham Phenomena." *Special Supplement: Hastings Center Report,* November to December (1994), S29-S32.

Frankel, R.M. "Emotion and the physician-patient relationship." *Motivation and Emotion,* 1995, 19: 163-173.

Fromer, Margot, Joan. *Ethical Issues in Health Care.* St. Louis: Mosby, 1981.

Glumgart, Hermann, L. "Caring For the Patient." *The New England Journal of Medicine.* Volume 270(9), (1964), 444-456.

Greenfield, S., S.H. Kaplan, and J.E. Ware. "Expanding patient involvement in care: Effects on patient outcomes." *Annals of Internal Medicine* 102: 520-8.

Hall, Judith, A., Dornan, Michael C. "What Patients Like About Their Medical Care and How Often They are asked: A Meta-Analysis of the Satisfaction Literature." *Social Science and Medicine, 1988,* 27(9), 935-939.

Hall, J.A., T.S. Stein, D.L. Roter, and N. Rieser. "Inaccuracies in physicians' perceptions of their patients." *Medical Care* 37: 1,164-8.

Hoffman, C., D. Rice, and H.Y. Sung. "Persons with chronic conditions: Their prevalence and costs." *Journal of the American Medical Association*, (1996), 276: 1,473-9.

Jackson, Jennifer. "Telling the Truth." *Journal of Medical Ethics*, (1991), 17, 5-9.

Kahneman, Daniel & Tversky, Amos. "Choices, Frames and Values." *American Psychologist*, (1984), Volume 39(4), 341-350.

Kantor, Jay. E. *Medical Ethics for Physicians-in-Training.* New York: Plenum Medical Book Company, 1989.

Kaufman, M.R. "Practising good manners and compassion." *Medical Insight,* (1970), 2: 56-61.

Kohut, Nitsa, Sam, Mehran O'Rourke, Keith MacFadden, Doublas K. Salit Irving, Singer, Peter A. "A stability of treatment preferences: although most preferences do not change, most people change some of their preferences." *Journal of Clinical Ethics.* (1997), Volume 8(2), 124-135.

Lee, Barbara, Coombs. *Compassion in Dying. Stories of Dignities and Choice.* Troutdale, Oregon: New Sage Press, 2003.

Lembke, Janet. *The Quality of Life: Living Well, Dying Well.* Guilford, Connecticut: The Lyons Press, 2003.

Levenstein, J.H. "The patient-centered general practise consultation." *South Africa Family Practice,* (1984), 5: 276-82.

Lewis, Rees, J. "Patient Views on Quality Care in General Practise: Literature Review." *Social Science and Medicine,* (1994), 39(5), 655-670.

Like, Robert, and Zyzanski, Stephen. "Patient Satisfaction with the Clinical Encounter: Social Psychological Determinants." *Social Science and Medicine,* 24(4), (1987), 351-357.

Lindemann, Nelson, Hilde, Lindemann Nelson James. "Prefrences and Other Moral Sources." *Special Supplement: Hastings Center Report.* November-December, (1994), S19-S20.

Lowenstein, Jerome. *The Midnight Meal and Other Essays about Doctors, Patients and Medicine.* Ann Arbor: The University of Michigan Press, 2005.

McCracken, E.C., M.A. Stewaret. J.B. Brown, and I.R. McWhinney. "Patient-centered care: The family practice model." *Canadian Family Physician,* (1983), 29: 2,313-16.

McCullough, Laurence and Christianson, Charles. "Ethical Dimensions of Diagnosis." *Metamedicine,* (1981), Volume 2, 129-141.

Miles, Steven, H. "Physician-Assisted Suicide and the Profession's Gyrocompass." *Hastings Center Report,1995,* May-June, 17-19.

Minogue, Brendan, P. and Taraszewski. "The Whole Truth and Nothing But the Truth?" *Hastings Center Report, 1988,* October-November, 34-36.

Morreim, Haavi. "Three Concepts of Patient Competence." *Theoretical Medicine,* 4 (1983), 231-252.

Niemira, Denise. "Life on the Slippery Slope: A Bedside View of Treating Incompetent Elderly Patients". *Hastings Center Report,* May-June (1993), 14-17.

Novack, Dennis, H., Detering Barbara, J., Arnold Robert Forrow, Lachlan Landinsky, Morissa, and Pezullo, John, C.

"Physicians Attitudes Toward Using Deception to Resolve Difficult Ethical Problems." *Journal of American Medical Association*, 261(20), (1989), 2980-2985.

Paasche-Orlow, Michael Roter Debra. "The Communication Patterns of Internal Medicine and Family Practise Physicians". *The Journal of the American Board of Family Practise*, 16 (2003), 485-493.

Payne, Sheila, Ellis-Hill, Caroline. *Chronic and Terminal Illness: New Perspectives on Caring and Careers*. Oxford: Oxford University Press, 2001.

Pearlman, Allan, Robert. "Are we asking the right questions?" *Special Supplement: Hastings Center Report*. November-December, (1994), S24-27.

Picard, Andre. *Matters of Life and Death*. British Columbia: Douglas & McIntyre, 2017

Ptacek, J.T., Eberhardt, Tara, L. "Breaking Bad News: A Review of the Literature." *The Journal of the American Medical Association*, 276(6), (1996), 496-502.

Randall, Fiona, Downie, R.S. *Palliative Care Ethics: A companion for all specialities*. Oxford: Oxford University Press, 1999.

Resnik, David, B., Rehm, Marsha, Minard, Raymond, B. "The Undertreatment of Pain: Scientific, Clinical, Cultural, and Philosophical Factors). *Medicine, Health Care and Philosophy*, (2001), 4: 277-288.

Robbins, Dennis, A. *Ethical Dimensions of Clinical Medicine*. Springfield, Thomas, 1981.

Rosenberg, James, E, and Toweres, Bernard. "The Practice of Empathy as a Prerequisite for Informed Consent." *Theoretical Medicine,* 7 (1986), 181-194.

Rothenberg. R.B., and J.P. Koplan. "Chronic disease in the 1990s." *Annual Review of Public Health,* (1990), 11: 267-96.

Shelp, Earl, E. *The Clinical Encounter: The Moral Fabric of the Patient-Physician Relationship.* Dordrecht: D. Reidel Publishing Company, 1983.

Sorbie, Anne. *Memoir of a Good Death.* Saskatoon, Saskatchewan: Thistle down Press, Ltd., 2010.

Spiro, Howard, M., Curnen Mccrea, Mary G. *Empathy and the Practice of Medicine: Beyond Pills and Scapel.* New Haven: Yale University Press, 1993.

Squier, R.W. "A model of emphatic understanding and adherence to treatment regimens in practitioner-patient relationships." *Social Science and Medicine,* 1990, 30: 325-39.

Stewart, Moira. "What is a Successful Doctor-Patient Interview? A Study of Interactions and Outcomes." *Social Science and Medicine,* 19(2), (1984), 167-175.

Stewart, Moira, Brown Judith Belle, Weston, Wayne, E., McWhinney, Ian R., McWilliam Carol, L., Freeman,

Thomas, R. *Patient-Centered Medicine: Transforming the Clinical Method.* London: Sage Publications, 1995.

Suchman, Anthony, L., Markakis, Kathryn, Beckman, Howard B., Frankel, Richard. "A Model of Empathic Communication in the Medical Interview." *Journal of the American Medical Association,* Volume 277(8), (1997), 678-682.

Sugarman, Jeremy. "Recognizing Good Decisionmaking for Incapacitated Patients." *Special Supplement: Hastings Center Report,* November-December, (1994), S11-S13.

Thom, David, H. and Campbell Bruce. "Patient-Physician Trust: An Exploratory Study." *The Journal of Family Practice,* (1997), 44(2), 169-176.

Tversky, Amos. "Elimination by Aspects." *Psychological Review, 1972,* Volume 79(4), 281-299.

Tversky, Amos, and Kahneman, Daniel. "The Framing of Decisions and the Psychology of Choice." *Science,* Volume 211, (1981), 453-458.

Tversky, Amos, and Kahneman, Daniel. "Judgement Under Uncertainty." *Science,* Volume 85, (1974), 1124-1131.

Veatch, Robert, M. "Abandoning Informed Consent." *Hastings Center Report,* March-April, (1995), 5-12.

Veatch, Robert, M. *A Theory of Medical Ethics.* New York: Basic Books, Inc., 1981.

Veatch, Robert, M. "Why Get Consent?" *Hospital Physician, 1975,* Volume 11, 30-31.

Volandes, Angelo, E. *The Conversation: A Revolutionary Plan for End-of-Life Care.* New York: Bloomsbury, 2015.

Wear, Stephen. *Informed Consent: Patient Autonomy and Clinician Beneficence within Health Care.* Washington, D.C.: Georgetown University Press, 1998.

Welie, Jos, V.M. Welie, Sander, P.K. "Patient Decision-Making Competence: Outlines of a Conceptual Analysis." *Medicine, Health Care and Philosophy,* (2001), 4, 127-138.

White, Peter. *Biopsychosocial Medicine: An Integrated Approach to Understanding Illness.* Oxford: Oxford University Press, 2005.

Wood, Sue and Pete Fox. *Dying: A Practical Guide for the Journey.* Wetton, Cape Town: Double Storey Books, 2005.

Wright, Richard, A. *Human Values in Health Care: The Practice of Ethics.* New York: McGraw Hill, 1988.